Woodbourne Library
Washington-Centerville Public Library
Centerville, Ohio

THE
BIG
BEAUTIFUL
BROWN RICE
COOKBOOK

THE WORLD'S BEST
BROWN RICE RECIPES

WENDY ESKO

D1219289

SQUAREONE
PUBLISHERS

Woodbourne Library
Washington-Centerville Public Library
Centerville, Ohio

COVER DESIGNER: Jeannie Tudor
COVER PHOTO: Getty Images
INTERIOR PHOTOS: Lundberg Family Farms
INTERIOR ILLUSTRATIONS: Vicki Chelf
EDITOR: Marie Caratozzolo
TYPESETTER: Gary A. Rosenberg

Square One Publishers
115 Herricks Road
Garden City Park, NY 11040
(516) 535–2010 • (877) 900-BOOK
www.squareonepublishers.com

The interior photographs that appear throughout this book have been reprinted with permission from the Lundberg Family Farms in Richvale, California.

Library of Congress Publisher's Cataloging-in-Publication Data

Esko, Wendy.
  The big beautiful brown rice cookbook : the world's best brown rice recipes / Wendy Esko.
    pages cm
  Includes index.
    ISBN 978-0-7570-0364-6 (pbk.)
    1. Cooking (Brown rice) 2. Cookbooks lcgft I. Title. II. Title: World's best brown rice recipes.
  TX809.B75E56 1973
  641.6'318—dc23

                                                                    2013017575

Copyright 2013 © by Wendy Esko

All rights reserved. No part of this publication may be reproduced, scanned, uploaded, stored in a retrieval system, or transmitted, in any form or by any means, electronic, mechanical, photocopying, recording, or otherwise, without the prior written permission of the copyright owner.

Printed in the United States of America

10 9 8 7 6 5 4 3 2 1

Contents

To Tomoko "Aveline" Kushi,
whose lifelong dream was to write a brown rice cookbook.
This book was originally inspired by Aveline,
and written with her in my thoughts.

Acknowledgments

I would like to thank the many people who have contributed to this book—both knowingly and unknowingly—beginning with the talented staff at Square One Publishers. Their dedication and hard work have made this book a reality. First and foremost, thanks to publisher Rudy Shur for his support and encouragement over the years in our many joint publishing ventures, and for his expertise and helpful suggestions. Special thanks goes to Marie Caratozzolo, whose expert editing and mastery of the English language show me at my very best. Through her expertise, she has not only brought focus to my thoughts and organization to my recipes, she has also taught me how to write a better book. I'd also like to acknowledge Vicki Chelf, artist, author, and vegan cook, for the step-by-step instructional drawings that accompany some of the more complex preparations in this book.

Thank you to all the farmers throughout the world, especially those who practice traditional and organic farming, whose vision, principles, dedication, and hard work supply us with the best possible food that keeps us healthy. I'd especially like to thank Lundberg Family Farms for not only growing the most delicious organic rice for decades, but also for graciously supplying the photos in this book. Special gratitude goes to Jordan Schultz at Lundberg for quickly and graciously responding to my photo request.

Special thanks to Helen Santelli, my first macrobiotic/natural foods cooking instructor, who served me my very first bowl of delicious brown rice. I have never forgotten that day, which forever changed the direction of my life. And to my friend and teacher Aveline Kushi, who, through the years, has introduced hundreds of thousands of people to the wonderful world of brown rice and other natural foods, as well as the art of macrobiotic cooking. Thank you to Michio Kushi, for his teachings, guidance, and encouragement over the years. I would also like to acknowledge my students, who have inspired me to study and more deeply understand the healing properties of food, and who are always challenging me to create new and tasty dishes. To my friends, who have dined at our home through the years, thank you for sharing your oohs and aahs, ideas, laughter, and presence.

I would like to thank my grandmother, Ruth Adelia Goodman Tyler, who patiently answered my countless questions, and let me stand by her side as a child while she gardened and cooked. She unknowingly inspired me to become the cook and avid gardener that I am today. To my parents, siblings, relatives, and many farmer ancestors, thank you for being part of the person I have become.

For never criticizing my food, and for always encouraging me to teach and write and write and then write some more, I want to thank Edward Esko. Finally, a heartfelt thanks to our children and grandchildren, who have served as my eager taste testers whenever I developed recipes for my classes and cookbooks. I always appreciated when they complained that I had not made enough. By watching them grow and interact, they have taught me more about the importance of healthy freshly made meals and about the kinds of food people like than any book or class ever could.

Preface

I was born and raised in the Finger Lakes region of New York State, where the rich soil and rolling hills are ideal for growing a wide variety of crops, including grains, beans, fruits, and vegetables. My family lived in the country surrounded by farms. Several of our neighbors grew wheat, oats, and barley. Year after year, I would take great delight in watching from our front lawn as they plowed, planted, and eventually harvested the grain. I watched for what seemed like forever for the first seeds to burst forth, producing tiny pale green sprouts. Slowly, the fields became a sea of deep green, growing taller with each passing day, until finally turning golden as the grain ripened and became ready for harvest.

One of the most beautiful images I remember is the wind blowing across the grain fields. The tall stalks, flexible and yielding, bowed down and then sprang back within seconds as if dancing in the field. This amazing performance, so peaceful and calming, always reminded me of the waves I had observed many times on nearby Lake Ontario as well as the Finger Lakes. Often, my siblings and I would walk along the edges of the fields, or play hide-and-seek in them, always knowing that soon our beautiful wonderland would be cut. As I grew older, I realized it was those golden fields that provided steaming bowls of creamy oatmeal on cold winter mornings, freshly baked breads and pastries, and rich and savory barley-vegetable soups.

As a child I loved grains, especially rice. (I can remember asking my mother for spoonfuls of my baby brother's rice cereal.) I always looked forward to her barley soups and to my grandmother's grain-stuffed cabbage rolls and sweet bell peppers. On Fridays, it was rare for me to be at home for dinner. Our neighbors, who were from the South, always served white rice on Friday, and often invited me to join them, knowing how much I loved their delicious Southern-style rice dishes.

It wasn't until I was in my twenties that I tasted brown rice for the first time. I was amazed at how different it was from white rice. Brown rice was naturally sweeter, much chewier, and, unlike white rice, it left me feeling totally satisfied after just one serving. I was truly impressed with this new-found grain. After attending a macrobiotic/natural foods cooking class in 1971, and learning of the nutritional advantages of brown rice, I began to make it a regular part of my meals.

In 1978, my husband, two young sons, and I journeyed to Japan. We delighted in watching rice being planted in the many small paddies around our Kyoto neighborhood. As we watched the planting, the sprouting of the grain, and the wind blowing across the golden fields of mature rice, it brought back those same images I had experienced as a child. We would observe the fields as if in meditation, so peaceful and calming. I remember feeling an overwhelming sense of gratitude to Nature and to the farmers who work so hard to provide food for not only my family, but also for families throughout the world.

While I still enjoy white rice from time to time, especially in sushi, light soups, and salads, it is brown rice that I have developed a true fondness for. When I am quietly sitting and enjoying a bowl of freshly cooked brown rice, I often find myself thinking, "This is the simplest, yet the most delicious and satisfying food I have ever eaten." Over the years, brown rice, along with other whole grains, legumes, vegetables, and fruit, have been the cornerstone of my family's diet. I am forever grateful for the good health these foods have given us.

There are hundreds of varieties of brown rice and many hundreds of ways to prepare and serve them. In this book I share just a sampling of these possibilities, beginning with the most basic methods. I think of these methods as notes on a musical scale from which hundreds of variations can be created. I hope you enjoy the recipes I have shared with you. I also hope you use them as springboards to create your own unique, delicious favorites that bring great health and happiness to you, your family, and your friends.

Introduction

*"*W*ould you like that with white rice or brown?"*

When restaurant patrons are offered this simple menu choice, all too often the brown rice that appears, while nutritionally superior to white, is bland and boring—far from a culinary treat. But brown rice can be as taste tempting and delectable as it is healthful. Through my macrobiotic background and decades of experience as a vegan/vegetarian/natural foods cook and cooking instructor, I know this to be true. And with *The Big Beautiful Brown Rice Cookbook,* you are about to discover it, too. In it, I have gathered together my favorite brown rice recipes—ones that have satisfied and delighted my family and friends over the years—and am truly happy to share this collection with you.

The book starts off with an informative chapter on brown rice basics. It contains a brief overview of this fascinating grain, including its history, nutritional profile, and significant role as a staple food throughout the world. Consider the remainder of this chapter a primer—a place to turn to when you have a question about the ingredients used in the recipes, or for guidance when shopping for and/or storing rice and other grains. An extensive glossary covers dozens of different rice varieties, the products made from this valuable grain, and much more. Clear cooking instructions will guide you in preparing rice perfectly, whether in a pot on the stove, in a pressure cooker, or with a rice cooker.

What follows next is a culinary brown rice adventure—one in which you will find dozens of fantastic kitchen-tested recipes that spotlight this nutritional powerhouse. Of the many hundreds of recipes I have accumulated over the years, I have chosen the best of the batch—from easy-to-make simple side dishes to sensational specialty fare. This book has it all.

Brown rice is incredibly versatile. For breakfast, you will find a variety of wonderful dishes to start your day. There are pancakes and waffles, creamy hot cereals, and crunchy breakfast bars to name just a few. And that's just the beginning. You will discover how brown rice can play the leading role in appetizers, like savory stuffed mushrooms and crunchy croquettes. Nothing is more comforting and satisfying than a bowl of homemade soup or a hearty stew, and the recipes I have chosen are those most requested by family and friends. Chapters devoted to salads, side dishes, and entrées offer both humble unadorned choices as well as show-stopping specialties. Included among them is a parade of regional classics and international delights—crisp samosas, savory falafel, stuffed grape leaves, and flavorful sushi, as well as stir-fries, paellas, risottos, curries, and so much more. And then there's dessert! This chapter offers delectable puddings, heavenly muffins, and even a recipe that shows you how to transform brown rice cakes into everyone's campfire favorite—s'mores.

To help ensure successful results, each recipe has easy-to-follow step-by-step reader-friendly directions, with instructional drawings for the more complex dishes. Helpful guidelines, tips, and suggestions are included as well. Finally, for your entertainment pleasure, you will find interesting bits of rice trivia and fascinating facts throughout.

If you've always thought that brown rice was dull, you're in for a real treat. It is my sincerest hope that *The Big Beautiful Brown Rice Cookbook* will show you how to create dishes that are not only delightfully delicious, but hearty and healthful as well. Get ready to discover all that this big beautiful grain has to offer.

Brown Rice Basics

Over the last generation, brown rice has become a staple in many households across North America and Europe. The health benefits of this ancient grain, which is the most widely used food crop on the planet, are now recognized by doctors and nutritionists worldwide. As the twenty-first century began, about 600 million metric tons of rice were being harvested annually around the world, nearly all for human consumption. (Although the amount of wheat and corn crops was slightly higher, much was used to feed livestock.) About 90 percent of the world's rice crop is grown and eaten in Asia—mostly in China, India, Indonesia, and Vietnam. For the nearly 3 billion people who live there, rice provides 25 to 80 percent of their daily calories.

Although much of the rice harvested today is processed and sold as white rice, the grain is brown in its natural state. A nutritionally complete whole grain, brown rice has not been milled or it has been partially milled, which simply means that it is not refined. Instead, only the *hull* or *husk*, the hard outer-most layer of the rice grain, is removed through a method known as *thrashing*. White rice is produced when the *bran* and the *germ* layers, which give rice its natural brown color, are also removed (through a method called *pearling*), and only the starchy *endosperm* remains. The parts of the rice grain are illustrated in the figure below.

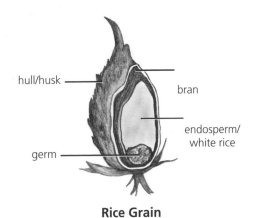

Rice Grain

Although white rice is later "enriched" to restore B vitamins and iron, these nutrients are usually derived from petrochemicals and animal sources. The bran and germ layers of whole grain brown rice naturally contain vitamins, minerals, dietary fiber, and essential fatty acids that are lost during processing—which is why brown rice is preferred.

I also encourage choosing organic brown rice. Not only does organically grown food taste better, it is also far more nutritious and free of contaminants like herbicides, pesticides, arsenic (from chemical fertilizers), and genetically modified organisms (GMOs). For more detailed information on GMOs, see the inset below. Eating organic brown rice ensures that you are reaping all of this simple food's natural, healthful benefits.

The recipes in this book introduce the many uses of brown rice, especially the short-grain variety. Because of its naturally sweet flavor and chewy texture, rice is the one grain that can be eaten daily in its whole form. And, since it is such a versatile food, it can serve as the basis for an endlessly varied healthful cuisine. In addition to a glossary of rice varieties and other ingredients used in the recipes found in this book, this chapter presents the simple cooking methods and basic equipment needed to transform this simple food into a wide range of delectable dishes. After reading this chapter, you'll have all you need to begin making your big, beautiful brown rice dishes.

AVOIDING GMOS

One of the many reasons organically grown food is recommended is that it means avoiding food that has been *genetically modified*. Genetically modified (GM) food comes from *genetically modified organisms* (GMOs). To put it simply, the genes of GM plants have been altered or artificially manipulated to mix and match the DNA of totally different species. Often this is done for the purpose of growing a bigger and supposedly better version of the crop, which is how GM crops are marketed. It is also done to create crops that are resistant to pesticides and herbicides. The crops can be doused with these chemicals, which kill weeds and pests, but do not harm the crops themselves. Genetically modified corn, for example, may look picture perfect and even taste good, but think about what you are actually eating. A plant that grows naturally would wither and die when doused with the same herbicide.

Recently, it has been proven that GM crops do not produce the higher yields that they were supposed to produce. Furthermore, raising genetically modified crops has resulted in the mutation of "super weeds" that are resistant to conventional herbicides and pesticides.

Concerns for human health and the environment are the most obvious reasons to avoid genetically modified foods. And people with food allergies need to be especially concerned as researchers are finding a growing number of links between the consumption of GM crops and the creation or worsening of allergies. One of the biggest fears is that splicing genes between two different species can inadvertently incorporate an allergenic protein into the modified crop or cause the formation of a new one.

Organic foods are our best assurance against genetically modified organisms, which is why it is best to choose them whenever possible. This is especially recommended when buying soybeans and corn and their derived products because nearly 60 percent of the corn and over 90 percent of the soybeans grown in the United States are genetically modified.

GLOSSARY OF INGREDIENTS

This glossary is designed to acquaint you with the healthful ingredients used in this book's recipes. Although not *every* ingredient is listed, it does include staple items, as well as some less common foods like sea vegetables and specialty rice varieties.

You can find most of the following items (preferably organic) in natural foods stores, which usually support local farmers, healthful food manufacturing practices, and sustainable agriculture. Farmers markets and online suppliers are other organic food sources, as are a growing number of local supermarkets. Just be sure to check food labels and try to choose products that are organic; and remember that foods and food products labeled "all natural" or "preservative free" does not necessarily mean they are organic or GMO free.

The list of Resources beginning on page 175 provides purchase information for the products that are lesser known and not always readily available.

Rice Varieties

Arborio rice. The name of this round, plump medium-grain rice comes from the name of the northwestern Italian town in which it is grown. Although white Arborio rice has a creamy consistency, the center of the grain stays firm, making it a popular choice for risotto. It also makes a good substitute for sushi rice. To maintain white Arborio's creamy consistency when making risotto, do not rinse it before cooking. When using it for sushi, rinse the grains thoroughly.) The chewier brown Arborio is well suited for making paella. Medium- or short-grain brown rice make good substitutes.

Basmati rice. This long-grain aromatic rice is grown in India and the United States. It is the most popular of the long-grain rice varieties due to its appealing aroma, flavor, and dry, fluffy texture. Basmati is available in both white and brown varieties. Brown basmati is more nutritious than white and has a crunchier texture and slightly nutty flavor.

Black Japonica rice. This spicy, aromatic rice blend was developed by California's Lundberg Family Farms by combining dark brown medium-grain mahogany rice with a black Japanese short-grain variety. It adds an exotic touch to many dishes, such as stuffings, stir-fries, salads, and grain burgers.

Brown rice, short-grain. Short-grain brown rice is the smallest and roundest of the brown rice varieties, with moist grains that stick together due to its glutinous quality. The hardiest of the brown varieties, short-grain brown rice has a naturally sweet taste and a balanced proportion of minerals, proteins, carbohydrates, and fats.

Brown rice, medium-grain. Medium-grain brown rice is slightly softer in texture than short-grain rice. It is also lighter and not quite as sweet or sticky. Fluffy and light when cooked, medium-grain varieties make excellent fried rice dishes.

RICE IS GLUTEN FREE

Although many rice varieties are sticky when cooked, this "glutinous" quality does not come from gluten—a protein factor to which some people are allergic. It comes from the starches—*amylase* and *amylopectin*—that are contained in its grains. Rice that is higher in amylopectin is shorter, stubbier, and sticky when cooked. Long-grain varieties are higher in amylase; when cooked, the grains are firm and tend to stay separated.

All rice is gluten free, making it a safe choice for those who are intolerant or allergic to wheat or other grains containing gluten.

Brown rice, long-grain. This is the lightest, least glutinous of the major varieties of brown rice due to its high amylase content. It has a chewier texture than white rice, but is firmer and fluffier than short-grain brown rice. Rich in fiber and B vitamins, this rice is ideally suited for pilafs, paellas, and stir-fries.

Brown rice, sweet. This short-grain brown rice is the stickiest, most glutinous of the rice varieties. It is also the sweetest. In Japan, sweet brown rice is traditionally used to make *mochi,* a sweet rice cake made by pounding the cooked grains into a thick, sticky paste. It is also used to make *ohagi,* a sticky rice patty that is coated with roasted soybean flour, chestnut purée, or crunchy ingredients like roasted ground walnuts, pecans, or sesame seeds. This rice is also used to make cookies, crackers, and dumplings for soup, as well as *amazake*—a sweet rice milk beverage.

Carnaroli rice. A hybrid, short-grain brown or white rice that is native to northern Italy, carnaroli has a very creamy texture (even creamier than Arborio), making it a good choice for risotto. Its plump grains are slightly larger than Arborio and hold their shape better. Carnaroli is often referred to as the "caviar of rice." In Italy, it is preferred over Arborio for making risotto due to its uniform starch-releasing qualities.

Countrywild rice. This Lundberg Family Farms exclusive blend of Wehani, long-grain brown, and black Japonica rice offers a great variety of tastes and textures.

Della rice. Native to Louisiana, Della rice is a hybrid of long-grain brown rice and aromatic basmati. When cooked, Della rice swells and becomes shorter and thicker than the basmati grain. It is best used in casseroles and pilafs. Long-grain brown rice, Texmati, and brown basmati all make good substitutes.

Golden Rose brown rice. Developed by the Lundberg Family Farms, this medium-grain specialty rice offers a nice balance between the light texture of long-grain brown rice with the chewy, moist texture of short-grain.

Jasmine rice. Considered Thailand's finest rice, long-grain aromatic jasmine is typically soft and slightly moist with a fragrant floral, nutty aroma and delicate texture. Also called *Thai fragrant rice,* jasmine rice is available in white and brown varieties. It is often used in Asian cuisine.

Jubilee rice. This colorful Lundberg Family Farms specialty blend is a combination of Wehani, Black Japonica, short- and medium-grain red rice, short- and long-grain brown rice, and sweet brown rice. This delicious variety of multiple grains is packed with flavor, texture, and added nutrition.

Red rice. This species of rice, originally from Asia and now grown in the United States, has an outer bran that is red in color. It has a characteristically firm, chewy texture that works well in salads and casseroles. The *Sri Lankan Red* variety has a mild flavor, cooks quickly, and is popular in seafood dishes. Another red rice variety—Lundberg Family Farm's short-grain *Christmas rice*—has a distinctive roasted nutty flavor. The cooked grains do not stick together, making this rice a nice choice for stuffings and puddings.

Texmati rice. This American variety of basmati rice is grown in Texas and the southern United States. It is a cross between basmati and Louisiana Della long-grain rice. It is not quite as aromatic as basmati, but like basmati, its grains stay separate when cooked.

Valencia rice. This Spanish-grown short- to medium-grain rice is traditionally used to make paella because of its slightly sticky consistency and tendency to easily separate when cooked. Unlike other short- and medium-grain varieties, Valencia is able to absorb moisture without breaking. This makes it a good choice for soups, stews, stuffings, croquettes, sushi, and rice pudding.

Wehani rice. This dark brown long-grain rice was developed by Lundberg Family Farms from a number of long-grain Indian basmati rice varieties. It has an aromatic nutty flavor and aroma, and is popular in stuffings, salads, and pilafs. When cooked, the grains split open like wild rice. Wehani rice is grown exclusively by Lundberg.

White rice. White rice is what remains after the nutrient-rich bran is removed from the whole grain. Although refined grains and grain products are generally not suggested for optimal health, they can be enjoyed for variety as occasional supplements to whole grains. Look for white rice that is organically grown and does not contain talc powder. Like brown rice, white rice comes in short-, medium-, long-grain, and glutinous varieties.

BUYING AND STORING GUIDELINES

As shown in the figure on page 3, brown rice (like all whole grains) contains an oil-rich germ that is covered by the outer bran. Because of this germ, rice can easily become rancid if it isn't stored properly. It is best to keep rice in a tightly sealed jar that is labeled with the type of rice that is inside along with the date. Although you can store the rice in the pantry, where it will keep for several weeks, keeping it in the refrigerator or freezer will ensure freshness for several months, especially in tropical climates. Rice and other grains will also keep for long periods in vacuum-sealed containers.

As I mentioned earlier, it is ideal to buy organic rice and grains whenever possible. It is also best to purchase rice that has not been stored for long periods of time. Shopping in stores with high turnover rates is one way to ensure that the rice and other products you buy are fresh. Always check expiration dates or "best if used by" dates on packages, and if you notice a rancid odor upon opening, throw the rice away. When buying in bulk, you can check the freshness of the rice by smelling it—the grain is freshest when it gives off a pleasant, almost sweet aroma. Buying high-quality organic grains is better for your health as well as your taste buds.

Some short-grain varieties are often referred to as "sticky" rice because they clump together when cooked.

Wild Blend. This Lundberg Family Farms exclusive product is a blend of Wehani, Black Japonica, long-grain brown rice, sweet brown rice, and wild rice. The multiple varieties offer a range of textures, flavors, and colors, as well as increased nutrition.

Wild pecan rice. A hybrid of basmati and Della, long-grain wild pecan rice is a product of the Cajun bayou rice-growing area of southern Louisiana. It has a nutty flavor and aroma with grains that are light, fluffy, and easily digestible, making it the perfect rice to serve as a simple side dish. It is also delicious with stir-fries, curries, and dishes like

Cajun red beans and rice. Brown basmati and Texmati are good substitutes for wild pecan rice.

Wild rice. Often referred to as a "pseudo grain," wild rice is actually a very tall, robust uncultivated aquatic grass and not a type of rice. It is often used in soups, stews, stuffings, puddings, and fried rice dishes. Much of what is sold as wild rice is actually cultivated paddy-grown rice that has been harvested and processed by machine—not true wild rice. Hand-harvested lake- and river-grown wild rice is authentic and far more flavorful and fluffy than the cultivated variety. You can find authentic wild rice in most natural foods stores. For a list of reliable sources, see the Resources beginning on page 175.

Other Grains and Grain Products

Amaranth. Small round amaranth seeds have a mild nutty flavor. They are gluten free, a good source of fiber, iron, protein, and calcium, and contain high levels of the essential amino acid lysine. Amaranth seeds require considerable chewing and are somewhat sticky, so this grain is not usually eaten as a side dish. More often, it is combined with brown rice or other grains, or added to soups, stews, pilafs, and puddings. Amaranth is also milled into flour.

Barley. Rich in fatty acids and stocked with vitamin E, thiamin, riboflavin, potassium, magnesium, iron, and the essential amino acid lysine, this nutty-flavored grain is lower in gluten than wheat, but still classified as a gluten-containing grain. It is also high in fiber, and light and chewy in texture. Barley also

takes many forms. *Whole barley* (also called *sprouting barley*) has its nutritious bran and germ layers intact. *Pearled barley*, which is typically found in supermarkets, is stripped of its nutrient-dense outer bran and germ, making it starchy, easy to chew, and faster to cook than all other varieties; but it is also much less nutritious. *Partially* or *semi-pearled barley*, available in most natural foods stores, has approximately 50 to 60 percent of its nutritious bran and germ layer intact. *Barley flour*, used to make pancakes, muffins, and other baked goods, is also available, as are cracked *barley grits*, which are often enjoyed as breakfast porridge. For longer freshness, barley grits, flakes, and flour should be stored in airtight containers and frozen or refrigerated. Whole and partially pearled varieties can be kept in a cool dark pantry.

Buckwheat groats. These whole, untoasted buckwheat grains are a rich source of fiber, calcium, iron, magnesium, potassium, and vitamins B and E. Groats can be toasted (*kasha*), which is stronger flavored than untoasted. They can also be cracked (*grits*). Untoasted groats are popular in pilafs, tabouli, stuffings, grain burgers, and croquettes, while toasted kasha makes a great a filling for knishes and stuffed cabbage. Groats can also be ground into flour. Contrary to its name, buckwheat is not a type of wheat nor is it related to wheat. It is a seed-bearing grass that is gluten free and classified as a "pseudo grain."

Kamut. Actually a trademarked brand for the ancient wheat known as *Khorasan*, Kamut is a relative of durum and can be substituted for wheat in most recipes. It is quick cooking and delicious when combined with brown rice. Although it contains gluten, Kamut is tolerated by some people with wheat intolerance. It is not, however, recommended for anyone with gluten intolerance or a true wheat allergy.

Millet. Millet is a sweet golden yellow grain whose seeds can make a tasty replacement for rice in many dishes. It is also delicious combined with rice or other grains. Millet is gluten free and easily digestible. It is also high in magnesium, protein, fiber, iron, and B vitamins. Millet's inedible outer hull is removed, but its nutrient-dense bran and germ are intact. Suitable as a main dish, millet is often added to croquettes, stuffings, pilafs, and soups; enjoyed as a hot breakfast cereal; or ground into flour and used to make pancakes and waffles.

Mochi. This sticky Japanese rice cake is made from pounded sweet rice, which is formed into blocks or sheets and dried. Small pieces can be pan-fried, baked, deep-fried, or cooked in a waffle iron. Mochi expands as it cooks, puffing up like a marshmallow and becoming crunchy on the outside and tender on the inside. When grated, mochi melts like cheese, making it a good cheese substitute on pizza, pasta, and certain soups like French onion. It is also good in lasagna and quesadillas. Fresh mochi is sometimes found in the dairy section of natural food stores. Dried mochi, which is vacuum packed for longer shelf life, is more commonly available. Like all rice products, mochi is gluten free.

Oats. A good source of cholesterol-reducing soluble fiber, manganese, selenium, tryptophan, magnesium, thiamin, and beneficial antioxidants, oats also promote good digestion. They can be be purchased as oat groats, steel-cut oats, or rolled oats. *Oat groats,* also called *oat berries,* are the whole grain variety and require soaking and longer cooking time. *Steel-cut oats* are groats that have been steamed, chopped, and roasted, and are often referred to as "Irish oatmeal" or "Scotch oats." Oats may also be steamed or roasted and flattened into flakes. These *rolled oats* cook quickly and are frequently used to make cookies, hot cereal, granola, and muesli. Rolled oats are also added to meatless loaves and croquettes, or ground into flour for pancakes, waffles, quick breads, and muffins. Although oats are gluten free, they are often grown near and/or stored near wheat, or processed on equipment that is also used for processing wheat. This is a concern for anyone on a gluten-free diet, who should purchase only oats that are "certified gluten free."

Quinoa. Although generally considered a grain, quinoa (pronounced *KEEN-wah*) is actually a seed that is related to amaranth. It is gluten free and a good source of beneficial fiber, magnesium, manganese, potassium, zinc, B vitamins, vitamin E, and calcium. Quinoa is one of the few "grains" that is a complete protein. It is available in white, red, and black varieties in North America, but many other varieties are available in South America. It cooks quickly and has a mild sweet to slightly bitter flavor. (Red quinoa is the sweetest.) All types can be enjoyed alone or combined with rice and other grains in pilafs, croquettes, salads, and soups. Quinoa is also delicious as a hot cereal.

Rye. A high-fiber cereal grain with an earthy flavor, rye is high in thiamin, selenium, and the essential amino acid lysine. Like wheat, rye is a gluten-containing grain. Rye berries are often enjoyed as a breakfast cereal or side dish. They are also delicious when combined with rice. Rye is mainly ground into flour and used to make bread and pasta.

Seitan. Often called "wheat meat," seitan (pronounced *SAY-tan*) is a meat substitute that is high in protein, low in fat, and cholesterol free. It is made by slow-simmering the gluten from whole wheat flour, which gives it a chewy meat-like texture. Like tofu, seitan absorbs the flavors of surrounding ingredients when cooked. It is less expensive than meat and can be a healthy replacement in most recipes. Seitan is available in the dairy section of most natural foods stores and a growing number of supermarkets.

Spelt. This nutty-tasting ancient grain of the wheat family is naturally high in fiber, protein, and B vitamins. Like any type of wheat, spelt can be enjoyed when combined with rice. Spelt flour is slightly sweeter than regular whole wheat flour, and can be substituted for wheat flour in most recipes. Although spelt contains gluten, it is tolerated by some people with wheat intolerance. It is not, however, recommended for anyone with gluten intolerance or a true wheat allergy.

Wheat. A versatile, fiber-rich grain, wheat is packed with protein, iron, magnesium, and B vitamins. Whole wheat berries can be cooked and eaten whole, sprouted, or ground into flour. Wheat, like all whole grains, is believed to play a role in reducing the risk of hypoglycemia, stroke, diabetes, coronary heart disease, and even some types of cancer. It's no wonder that wheat is a staple grain throughout the world. Wheat varieties are classified as soft or hard. Soft varieties are low in gluten and high in starch. Flour made from soft wheat (pastry flour) is good for making biscuits, pastry dough, cookies, and other products that are meant to be crumbly. Because hard wheat varieties are higher in gluten, the flour is better suited for bread, pasta, and products like seitan. Durum wheat is the hardest type and the best choice for making the very stiff dough needed for dried pasta.

Beans and Soyfoods

Azuki beans. Commonly used in macrobiotic and Japanese cooking, azuki beans (also called *aduki* or *adzuki*) are high in both protein and fiber. They are also lower in fat and more digestible than most other bean varieties.

Azukis are dark red in color and comparable in size to navy and mung beans. They are grown in the United States and several Asian countries with the most flavorful variety from Hokkaido, Japan.

Black beans. Also called *Mexican black* or *black turtle beans*, these small, oval-shaped legumes have a shiny appearance and distinct flavor. Like all beans, black beans are a good source of fiber, protein, and important nutrients such as B vitamins, iron, zinc, and calcium. They are popular in countless Latin American and Caribbean dishes, and are often added to soups and stews or served over rice.

Black-eyed peas. These legumes get their name from their distinctive appearance—they are creamy-white in color with a small black spot resembling an eye. Black-eyed peas are rich in fiber and potassium, and a good source of zinc and iron. A food staple in the southern United States, black-eyed peas are very versatile and a popular addition to soups, stews, and rice dishes. When tossed into salads, they are sometimes referred to as "Texas caviar." Traditionally served during Kwanza, black-eyed peas are also prepared with rice and greens in a West African-inspired stew called Hoppin' John. Many believe that eating this stew on New Year's Day before noon will bring a year of good luck.

Chickpeas. Also known as *garbanzo* or *ceci beans*, this Middle Eastern and Indian staple is rich in protein, fiber, and iron. Whole chickpeas are often added to soups, salads, curries, and stews, or ground and used to make falafel patties and hummus.

Edamame. A culinary staple in China and Japan, these protein-rich immature green soybeans (pronounced *eh-dah-MAH-may*) are gaining popularity in the United States. Although they are generally sold in the pod, only the beans themselves are edible. Edamame are often boiled and enjoyed as snacks (the beans are typically squeezed from the pod and popped directly into the mouth). When shelled, they can substitute for green peas and lima beans in any recipe.

Great Northern beans. Rich in protein and fiber, these medium-sized white beans are an excellent source of magnesium, iron, and folate. Naturally mild in taste, Great Northern beans are delicious in chili, casseroles, soups, and salads. They can also be mashed and enjoyed in dips and spreads. Navy, cannellini, and other white beans are good substitutes for Great Northern, although the cooking time, flavor, and texture will be slightly different.

Kidney beans. Light red, dark red, or white in color, kidney beans are staples of traditional Caribbean, Latin American, and Mediterranean cooking. The white variety, also known as

A WORD ABOUT BEANS

Delicious nutrient-rich beans/legumes are the perfect complement to rice and other grain dishes. When eaten together, beans and grains offer complete protein. Preparing dried beans from scratch is ideal; however, there may be days when you simply don't have the time or the desire to do so. For those times, cooked beans, which come in cans or glass jars, are a quick, convenient option.

When purchasing prepared bean varieties, try to opt for organic, which are GMO and pesticide free. Also look for those packed in cans with linings that are free of bisphenol A (BPA), an industrial chemical present in many hard plastic bottles and metal food and beverage cans. BPA has been implicated in a growing number of health concerns. Cans with BPA-free linings will have this clearly stated on the labels.

Italian white or *cannellini beans*, are preferred for traditional minestrone and other Italian classics. All kidneys are meaty in texture and popular additions to salads, soups, stews, and brown rice dishes. They also make great refried beans, dips, and sandwich spreads.

Lentils. Small, round, and somewhat flat, lentils are available in red, green, yellow, brown, and black varieties. They cook more quickly than most other beans and don't require soaking. Lentils make great additions to soups, stews, croquettes, casseroles, meatless loaves, and grain burgers. They also make delicious dips and pâtés. Lentils are often used in dal—a thick, spicy Indian stew. Green, brown, and black lentils are especially delicious when combined with brown rice.

Mung beans. These small round green beans are high in protein, iron, and potassium, and often used in traditional Indian cooking. Sprouted mung beans are popular in Asian cuisine. When milled into flour, they are used to make the translucent Asian noodles called *harusame.* They are an excellent source of vitamin C and a popular addition to soups, stir-fries, and brown rice dishes.

Natto. Made from fermented soybeans, natto is popular in Japan, where it is traditionally eaten as an easily digestible breakfast food. It is also commonly seasoned with soy sauce and mustard and served over rice or noodles, or used as a filling for vegetarian sushi rolls. Rich in protein, vitamin B_{12}, and vitamin K, natto is believed to be beneficial for heart health. It should not be confused with "natto miso," which is a sweet and salty miso chutney.

Pinto beans. These medium-sized beans are rosy-beige with brownish-red speckles. They are popular in Caribbean, Latin American, South American, and Native American cuisines. Pinto beans are eaten whole, mashed, or refried. Their deliciously rich, mildly sweet flavor makes them a terrific addition to salads, soups, stews, dips, salsas, and dishes like Spanish rice and other brown rice creations.

Soybeans. A principal crop of eastern Asia for thousands of years, yellow soybeans are now consumed around the world in both their whole and processed forms. They are the source of a variety of natural foods, including tofu, tempeh, soymilk, miso, natto, and shoyu and tamari soy sauce. Soybeans are high in protein; essential fatty acids (EFAs), especially omega-3; vitamins; minerals; and beneficial soy isoflavones. Black soybeans, which are lower in fat and sweeter than the yellow variety, are often cooked with brown rice. Because the majority of soybeans grown in the United States contain genetically modified organisms (GMOs), always try to choose organic varieties.

Tempeh. Made from cooked and fermented soybeans, tempeh (pronounced *TEM-pay*) is a tender, cake-like product that is rich in fiber, protein, calcium, magnesium, riboflavin, and iron. Tempeh, which comes in many flavors and varieties, must be cooked before it is eaten. It is a great choice for sandwiches, and can also be diced or cubed and added to rice and other grain dishes, pasta, or vegetable salads. It is available in the frozen food or dairy section of most natural foods stores.

Land and Sea Vegetables

Burdock. This long, narrow, carrot-shaped root vegetable has a brown skin and cream-colored interior. Available in most large natural foods stores and Asian markets, this edible root is a good source of fiber, calcium, potassium, and amino acids. Great in soups and stews.

Chestnuts, dried. Available in many natural foods stores and Asian markets, dried chestnuts are delicious cooked with brown rice or sweet brown rice.

Daikon radish. Resembling a long, round white carrot, this vegetable is commonly used in Asian cooking, both raw and cooked. Raw daikon is often sliced or grated and added to salads; it can also be pickled. Cooked daikon is popular in soups, stews, and stir-fries. It is also available shredded and dried, which is sweeter than fresh.

Dandelion greens. Typically thought of as pesky lawn weeds, dandelion greens are highly nutritious and may be eaten cooked or raw. Young tender greens are best (older greens tend to be bitter) and can be added raw to salads, or cooked and enjoyed as a side dish.

Kombu. This wide, thick sea vegetable is a type of edible kelp that is loaded with nutrients, including calcium, potassium, iodine, vitamin A, B vitamins, and trace minerals. Usually sold dried in flat strips, kombu has a mild salty taste and is used mainly as a flavoring agent in soup stock. Small pieces may be added to a pot of beans during cooking or used to flavor slow-cooking soups and stews. A small piece can also be used instead of sea salt when cooking brown rice or other grains. It is best to purchase kombu from a natural foods store, as many varieties sold in Asian markets have been sprayed with monosodium glutamate (MSG) as a softening agent.

Lotus root. Popular in southern and eastern Asia, this nutrient-rich root is from a type of water lily. Fresh lotus root has a mildly sweet, starchy taste and crunchy texture that is often compared to a water chestnut. It can be cut into slices and eaten raw, deep-fried, or baked into crunchy chips; or diced and added to grain dishes, soups, stews, and stir-fries. Lotus root slices are also available dried. When reconstituted, they are a delicious addition to grains, soups, and vegetables dishes.

Maitake. Grown in Japan and the United States, this firm, fleshy, succulent mushroom has a delicate earthy flavor and chewy texture. It is also known as *hen of the woods* because one maitake stem sprouts several caps, giving it the appearance of a fluffed-up feathered hen. It is delicious in grain dishes, as well as soups, stews, and sauces.

Nori. Lowest in sodium of all the sea vegetables, nori ranges in color from dark green to deep purple. It is usually pressed into thin sheets and dried. Toasted sheets are used as wrappers for rolled sushi and Japanese rice balls. Nori flakes are commonly used as a garnish or condiment.

Shiitake. This most popular Japanese mushroom has a delicate woodsy flavor. Available fresh and dried, shiitake have broad umbrella-shaped caps and inedible fibrous stems. They can be enjoyed raw, although cooking enhances their flavor. Fresh shiitake are delicious grilled or sautéed. Dried varieties are often simmered in soups and stews and are delicious in grain dishes, sauces, and gravies.

Snow peas. These flat green pods are crisp, tender, and sweet. Delicious raw, snow peas are a favorite addition to salads. They are also great in stir-fries and other Asian-style dishes. Tender snap peas can be substituted for snow peas in most dishes.

Watercress. This mildly pungent green is a member of the mustard family. Its dark green leaves have a slightly bitter, peppery flavor and are often added raw to salads or sandwiches. Watercress contains significant amounts of iron, calcium, and folic acid, as well as vitamins A, C, and E.

Winter squash. There are many varieties of hard winter squash, including acorn, butternut, buttercup, delicata, sweet dumpling, blue and green Hubbard, Hokkaido pumpkin, red kuri, spaghetti, and more. All have hard rinds and flesh that is usually orange in color and sweet in flavor when cooked. They are high in fiber, potassium, iron, vitamins A, B, and C, and omega-3 fatty acids.

Seasonings, Flavor Enhancers, and Thickeners

Bonito flakes. Known as *katsuo-boshi* in Japan, these dried, pinkish-tan shavings come from aged bonito fish, a type of mackerel. They have a savory smoky flavor and are used to make soup stocks, garnish noodle dishes, and season salads and sauces.

Kuzu. The starchy powdered root of the kuzu (or *kudzu*) plant is used as a thickening agent in stews, sauces, gravies, custards, pie fillings, jams, and jellies. In Japan, kuzu is also used as a home remedy for alleviating digestive problems. Unlike arrowroot, kuzu has no perceptible taste. Its thickening properties are also superior to arrowroot and cornstarch. It is best to purchase pure kuzu from a natural foods store to avoid varieties that have been diluted with genetically modified and/or chemically processed additives like potato starch or cornstarch.

Mirin. This sweet rice cooking wine is brewed like sake but has a lower alcohol content. In Japanese and macrobiotic cooking, mirin is an essential ingredient in sushi rice. It is also used to sweeten sauces and add a glaze to pastries, pie crusts, and breads.

Miso. This fermented soybean paste is made from steamed soybeans, cultured grains, and salt. A staple food in Japan, miso is used to flavor soups, stews, pâtés, dips, salad dressings, and marinades. The flavor of miso varies depending on the bean or grain that is used and the length of fermentation. Light-colored misos have a mild taste that makes them ideal for cream sauces, light soups, marinades, and salad dressings, while darker misos have a stronger, saltier flavor that is well-suited for hearty soups, stews, casseroles, and some grain dishes. Look for traditionally fermented, organic varieties, as most commercial misos are artificially fermented, made with genetically modified soybeans, and may contain monosodium glutamate (MSG).

Pickled ginger. Typically served with sushi and used as a palate cleanser, these thin slices of ginger are blanched and then pickled in rice vinegar, salt, and sweetener (naturally malted rice or barley syrup). Red shiso leaves give the ginger a rosy pink color. Natural pickled ginger, which is available in natural foods stores, is recommended. Avoid products that are sweetened with refined sugar and get their color from artificial red dye.

Sea salt. Made from evaporated seawater, sea salt is a healthful alternative to table salt. Because it is unrefined, sea salt is richer in trace minerals, lower in sodium chloride, and generally free of additives.

Shiso leaves. Also called *perilla*, shiso is an herb that has characteristic green or red ruffled leaves. Fresh green leaves are used mainly for garnishing sushi, while the red are used to give umeboshi plums, ume vinegar, and pickled ginger their rosy red color. Red shiso leaves are rich in beta carotene and antioxidants; can be eaten raw, cooked, or pickled; and are frequently added to salads, soups, and rice dishes. Pickled, dried, and finely ground red shiso is sold in natural foods stores as a condiment that is sprinkled on rice and other grain dishes, pasta, and vegetables.

Shoyu. This natural soy sauce, which is native to Japanese culture, is made from a combination of soybeans, water, cracked wheat, and sea salt. To avoid brands that contain chemicals, preservatives, genetically modified organisms (GMOs), and other undesirable ingredients, always choose organic, naturally fermented shoyu.

Tamari. This natural Japanese soy sauce is actually the dark liquid that rises to the top of fermenting vats of miso. Today, most tamari is brewed in a similar manner to shoyu (the other notable and most frequently used Japanese soy sauce). Unlike shoyu, tamari is wheat free, making it a good choice for those with wheat allergies. It is also darker in color and richer in flavor than shoyu, but tends to discolor and darken any food to which it is added. Tamari is the more common choice in food production—as a glaze on chips and crackers, for example—and for longer-cooked dishes. Shoyu is the preferred table and finishing soy sauce for everyday cooking. Always choose organic, naturally fermented tamari. Avoid brands that contain chemicals, preservatives, genetically modified organisms (GMOs), and other undesirable ingredients.

Umeboshi. This salty pickled plum is frequently used to flavor sauces, salad dressings, dips, cooked vegetable dishes, sushi rolls, and rice balls. Umeboshi are used whole, chopped, or ground into a paste. Traditional varieties found in natural foods stores, which are flavored with sea salt and colored with red shiso leaves, are recommended. Avoid brands that contain chemicals, preservatives, and artificial food colorings.

A Little Rice Trivia . . .

Rice is the main dietary staple for over half the world's population.

PREPARING TO COOK

Before presenting instructions on how to cook rice, it's important to first discuss some preliminary preparation guidelines. Follow these simple suggestions for the best-tasting results.

When preparing rice, fresh spring water or filtered tap water is best. Distilled water is not recommended as it is devoid of important minerals. You can buy quality spring water at natural foods stores. You can also filter your tap water. A number of excellent water filter units are available.

For added taste and easier digestibility, a pinch of salt can be added to the rice at the beginning of cooking. Unrefined sea salt, which is rich in trace minerals and free of added chemicals, is recommended. Instead of sea salt, you can add a small piece of kombu—a mildly salty, mineral-rich sea vegetable—to the pot.

Before cooking rice, spread out the grains on a plate and remove any hulls or small stones. (They will be easier to spot on a light-colored plate). Place the rice in a bowl and cover with cold water. Swish the rice around with your hand, pour off the water, and repeat once or twice. Some grains are dustier than others and may require repeated rinsing. Transfer the rice to a strainer and rinse under cold water. It is now ready to be cooked.

Optional Preparations

Although it isn't necessary, after rinsing and draining the rice, you can choose to either roast it or soak it before cooking. Both options require very little effort, and result in subtle differences in taste and texture.

Roasting

Roasting the rice before cooking produces grains that are dry, fluffy, and slightly nutty tasting. Simply heat a heavy stainless steel or cast iron skillet over high heat and add the rinsed rice. (For even roasting and to prevent burning, it is best to do this in small batches.) Stir the grains constantly until most of the water has evaporated. This usually takes anywhere from three to five minutes, depending on the quantity and type of rice. Once the grains are dry, reduce the heat to low and continue to stir for four to five minutes or until they release a nutty fragrance and turn slightly golden. (Be careful not to burn.) The roasted grains are now ready to cook.

Soaking

Soaking the rice before cooking results in grains that are plumper, softer, easier to chew and digest, and sweeter than grains that are not. It also shortens cooking time from one-quarter to one-half the time it takes to cook unsoaked grains. Japanese researchers discovered that soaking rice prior to cooking improves its digestibility and increases availability of its nutritional content.

For a *traditional soak*, place the rinsed rice in a bowl, stainless steel pot, or pressure cooker, and cover with the amount of cold water called for in the recipe. Cover (to keep out any dust) and let sit for six to eight hours. The rice is now ready to cook right in the soaking water. For a *quick soak*, follow the same procedure, but cut the soaking time to anywhere from thirty to sixty minutes.

COOKING METHODS

The two most popular methods for preparing rice are stovetop cooking and pressure cooking. As you will see, both methods are very simple and practically foolproof. Keep in mind that cooking times and the amount of water needed will vary depending on the type of rice, as well as the cooking method. This specific information is provided in two tables: "Cooking Rice on a Stovetop" (page 19) and "Cooking Rice in a Pressure Cooker" (page 20).

Stovetop Cooking

Cooking rice in a covered pot on the stove is arguably the most popular method. Although it involves slightly more attention than cooking rice in a pressure cooker, it is very easy and doesn't require a special appliance. All you need is a heavy pot with a tight-fitting lid, which is best for retaining heat and moisture, and results in rice that is evenly cooked. I prefer pots made of stainless steel. They are durable, easy to clean, and reasonably priced. As far as pot size, it must be big enough to allow the rice to expand—most varieties double or triple in volume when cooked. It should not, however, be too large or the rice won't cook properly. Do not, for instance, cook one cup of rice in a four-quart pot.

There are two basic types of stovetop burners—gas and electric. Most people prefer cooking with gas because it offers several advantages over electric. The flame on a gas burner ignites instantly and its heat level can be adjusted quickly. The heat is also more evenly distributed.

Conversely, the burners on an electric stovetop take time to heat up and cool down. When cooking rice, the problem is that once the ingredients come to a boil, the heat needs to be reduced immediately. (See the Basic Stovetop Cooking Directions below.) This type of heat adjustment cannot be done quickly on an electric stovetop.

There is, however, something you can do to overcome this drawback. Place the pot on a burner over high heat. When the ingredients are almost ready to come to a boil, turn another burner on low heat. Once the ingredients have come to a boil, transfer the pot to the burner with low heat. The temperature change will be immediate, as required for best results.

BASIC STOVETOP COOKING DIRECTIONS

1. Place the rinsed grains in a pot along with the required amount of cooking water and bring to a boil over high heat.

2. Add a small two-finger pinch of sea salt or a 1-inch square of soaked kombu to the pot.

3. Cover and reduce the heat to medium-low. Simmer for the required time or until the grains are tender.

4. Remove the pot from the heat (leave covered) and let sit for five to ten minutes.

5. Uncover the pot, fluff the rice with a fork, and serve.

COOKING RICE ON A STOVETOP

When cooking rice in a pot on the stove, use the following table to determine the amount of water, cooking times, and the approximate yields of various rice varieties. Follow the "Basic Stovetop Cooking Directions" on page 18. Keep in mind that the following information is *approximate,* and based on unsoaked/unroasted grains.

RICE TYPE (1 CUP)	WATER AMOUNT	COOKING TIME	APPROXIMATE YIELD
Arborio, brown	2 cups	45 to 50 minutes	3 cups
Arborio, white	1½ cups	20 minutes	2½ cups
Basmati, brown	2 cups	45 to 50 minutes	3 cups
Basmati, white	1½ cups	15 minutes	2½ cups
Black Japonica*	2 cups	45 to 50 minutes	3 cups
Brown, short-grain	2 cups	50 minutes	3 cups
Brown, medium-grain	2 cups	50 minutes	3 cups
Brown, long-grain	2 cups	50 minutes	3 cups
Brown, sweet	2 cups	50 minutes	3 cups
Carnaroli, brown	2 cups	50 minutes	3 cups
Carnaroli, white	1½ cups	20 minutes	2½ cups
Countrywild*	2 cups	50 minutes	3 cups
Della	1½ cups	20 minutes	2½ cups
Golden Rose*	2 cups	50 minutes	3 cups
Jasmine, brown	2 cups	50 minutes	3 cups
Jasmine, white	1½ cups	15 minutes	2½ cups
Jubilee*	2 cups	50 minutes	3 cups
Red	2 cups	50 minutes	3 cups
Sushi, white	1½ cups	20 minutes	2½ cups
Texmati	2 cups	50 minutes	3 cups
Valencia	1½ cups	20 minutes	2½ cups
Wehani*	2 cups	45 minutes	3 cups
White (long-, medium- or short-grain)	1½ cups	15 to 20 minutes	2½ cups
Wild	2½ cups	50 minutes	3 cups
Wild Blend*	2 cups	50 minutes	3 cups
Wild pecan	1¼ cups	15 minutes	2½ cups

* Specialty rice/rice blend from Lundberg Family Farms.

COOKING RICE IN A PRESSURE COOKER

When cooking rice in a pressure cooker, use the following table to determine the amount of water, cooking times, and the approximate yields of various rice varieties. Follow the "Basic Pressure-Cooking Directions" on page 21. Keep in mind that preparing at least two cups of rice in a pressure cooker is recommended for the best results. Also keep in mind that the following information is *approximate,* and based on unsoaked/unroasted grains.

RICE TYPE (1 CUP)	WATER AMOUNT	COOKING TIME	APPROXIMATE YIELD
Arborio, brown	1½ cups	25 minutes	2½ cups
Arborio, white	2 cups	10 minutes	2 cups
Basmati, brown	1½ cups	25 minutes	2½ cups
Basmati, white	1 cup	10 minutes	2½ cups
Black Japonica*	1½ cups	25 minutes	2½ cups
Brown, short-grain	1½ cups	25 minutes	2½ cups
Brown, medium-grain	1½ cups	25 minutes	2½ cups
Brown, long-grain	1½ cups	20 minutes	2½ cups
Brown, sweet	1½ cups	25 minutes	2½ cups
Carnaroli, brown	1½ cups	25 minutes	2½ cups
Carnaroli, white	1 cup	10 minutes	2 cups
Countrywild*	1½ cups	25 minutes	2½ cups
Della	1¼ cups	10 minutes	2 cups
Golden Rose*	1½ cups	25 minutes	2½ cups
Jasmine, brown	1½ cups	25 minutes	2½ cups
Jasmine, white	1 cup	10 minutes	2 cups
Jubilee*	1½ cups	25 minutes	2½ cups
Red	1½ cups	20 minutes	2½ cups
Sushi, white	1¼ cups	10 minutes	2½ cups
Texmati	1½ cups	25 minutes	2½ cups
Valencia	1 cup	10 minutes	2 cups
Wehani*	1½ cups	25 minutes	2½ cups
White (long-, medium- or short-grain)	1 cup	10 minutes	2 cups
Wild	1¼ cups	20 minutes	2½ cups
Wild Blend*	1½ cups	25 minutes	2½ cups
Wild pecan	1 cup	10 minutes	2 cups

* Specialty rice/rice blend from Lundberg Family Farms.

Pressure-Cooking

One of the most obvious advantages of using a pressure cooker—an airtight pot that steams the rice "under pressure" at high temperatures—is that it cuts down cooking time. It also allows the grains to retain more nutrients. Pressure-cooking is ideal for preparing brown rice that is combined with other longer-cooking grains (whole barley, wheat, Kamut, spelt, rye, whole oats) and soaked dried beans. Cooking two cups or more is recommended for the best results.

Pressure cookers are available in a variety of models. I prefer those made of stainless steel rather than enamel, which can chip and scratch easily. Not only are stainless steel cookers easy to clean, they have thick plates at the base for better heat dispersion, which results in even cooking. Avoid cookers made of aluminum, which has been linked to a number of health risks, and can leach into the food. Today, most models have several built-in safety mechanisms and are much safer and far easier to use than older models.

When using a pressure cooker, be sure to follow the operating instructions carefully for your particular model. Although the cooking times and instructions will vary, all cookers follow the same basic steps, which are presented in the inset at right.

When cooking rice in a pressure cooker on a gas stove, I recommend using a *flame deflector*. Also called a *flame tamer*, this light round metal or cast iron disc is placed on top of the stovetop burner under the pressure cooker. It elevates the cooker slightly and helps evenly distribute the heat from the flame below. The rice cooks more evenly and the likelihood of scorched rice at the bottom of the cooker is greatly reduced.

BASIC PRESSURE-COOKING DIRECTIONS

1. Place the rinsed grains in the cooker along with the required amount of cooking water (do not fill more than two-thirds).

2. Add a small two-finger pinch of sea salt or a 1-inch square of soaked kombu sea vegetable to the pot.

3. Put the cover on the cooker and place on the stovetop over high heat until it comes to full pressure (according to the operating manual).

4. Reduce the heat to low or medium-low—just enough to maintain pressure. Begin timing at this point.

5. At the end of cooking time, remove the pot from the heat and allow the pressure to come down on its own (about five or ten minutes). Remove the cover, spoon out the rice, and serve.

Using a Rice Cooker

In addition to cooking rice in a pot on the stove or in a pressure cooker, using a rice cooker is another viable option. This is an especially good choice for those with little time and/or cooking skills. It is also good for anyone who doesn't have access to a stove.

Rice cookers are available in many makes and models and come with various features. Choose one with a stainless steel insert for optimum results. Each cooker comes with a special measuring cup that is not the same size as a standard US measuring cup (240 ml or 1 cup). It is a "cup" according to rice cooker industry standards (180 ml or about ¾ cup). For this reason, it is important to follow manufacturer cooking instructions, or make the necessary adjustments if using a standard measuring cup.

One drawback of a rice cooker involves herbs and spices, which tend to clump together during cooking. To prevent this from happening, it is necessary to first mix the seasonings in the liquid before adding them to the pot. This will allow for more even distribution of the seasonings throughout the grains during cooking.

One of the benefits of rice cookers is that most models come with automatic timers that let you know when the rice is ready. Many also keep the rice warm after it is cooked. Along with rice, you can use most cookers to prepare other grains, as well as porridge, rice and bean combinations, soup, and more.

COOKING BROWN RICE WITH OTHER GRAINS

Combining short-, medium-, or long-grain brown rice with other grains results in a delectable variety of flavors and textures. Some grains, such as amaranth, teff, quinoa, and buckwheat, add a mild bitter flavor to the dish, while others, like fresh sweet corn, sweet brown rice, millet, and whole oats, lend a mildly sweet taste. Grains like whole barley, rye, and wheat (including Kamut and spelt) give rice dishes a wonderful chewy texture. Combining grains with brown rice also adds extra protein, minerals, beneficial fiber, B vitamins, and other nutrients.

When determining the amount of rice and other grains to use when preparing combination dishes, the usual proportion is ¾ cup brown rice to ¼ cup of the other grain. You can also use equal portions, if desired.

Harder grains, such as whole wheat, Kamut, spelt, rye, whole barley, and whole oats, need to be soaked and parboiled before they are cooked with brown rice, which requires less cooking time. After rinsing the grains, place them in a bowl and cover with cold water. Let soak for six to eight hours, then transfer them along with the soaking water to a heavy pot. Parboil for an hour or two, or until the grains are nearly tender. Now they can be added to the brown rice during cooking. You can also cook the grains completely, and then simply mix them together with the cooked rice.

When pressure-cooking harder grains with brown rice, place them along with the rice in the pressure cooker. Add the correct water measurement for the combined total of rice and grain (approximately $1\frac{1}{2}$ cups of water per cup of rice/grain combination), and let soak for six to eight hours. Pressure-cook the soaked ingredients according to the specific cooker instructions.

Grains that do not require soaking include millet, partially pearled barley, all types of quinoa, buckwheat, teff, amaranth, and all rice varieties—short-, medium-, and long-grain brown rice; sweet brown rice; wild rice; and white rice.

COOKING BROWN RICE WITH BEANS

Combining brown rice with beans (legumes) creates a rich, satisfying, and even more nutritionally complete dish than rice alone. When whole grains and beans are cooked together, they offer complete protein, supplying all of the essential and non-essential amino acids.

For this reason, eating these combination dishes often—at least two or three times a week—is suggested.

Dried beans usually require longer cooking time than grains, and often need advance preparation. With the exception of lentils, split peas, mung beans, and black-eyed peas, dried beans benefit from presoaking, which makes them softer and easier to digest.

After rinsing the beans, place them in a bowl with enough cold water to cover and let soak for six to eight hours. Drain the soaked beans and then rinse. (When preparing azuki beans, you can use the soaking liquid as part of the water measurement called for in the recipe. The soaking liquid for all other bean varieties should be discarded.) Transfer the beans to a heavy pot along with three to four cups of fresh water per cup of beans. Bring to a boil, reduce the heat to medium-low, and cover the pot. Simmer gently (rapid boiling will cause them to burst) and cook until tender yet slightly firm—this will take anywhere from thirty minutes to three hours, depending on the size and hardness of the bean. Drain the beans and allow them to cool slightly before adding them to the brown rice for cooking. You can also cook the beans until completely tender, then simply combine them with the cooked brown rice.

If using a pressure cooker, first soak the beans as instructed in the previous paragraph. Drain the soaked beans, rinse, and place them in the pressure cooker along with the brown rice. Add the correct water measurement for the combined total of rice and soaked beans (approximately $1^1/_2$ cups of water per cup of rice/bean combination), and any seasonings. Pressure-cook according to cooker instructions.

To always have cooked beans on hand, I usually prepare a few different varieties, and then store them in the refrigerator where they will keep up to a week. The quickest option, of course, is to use organic canned beans, preferably in BPA-free cans. Simply drain the canned beans, rinse, and then use as desired.

SUMMING IT UP

Now you have all the basics you need to get started. The recipes in this book will help you create dishes that are not only surprisingly delicious, but also hearty and healthful. Get ready to discover all the goodness that brown rice has to offer.

A Little Rice Trivia . . .

Rice is the highest yielding cereal grain (one seed yields over 3,000 grains).

2

Breakfast Dishes

Brown rice dishes for breakfast? Absolutely! It's no secret that breakfast is considered the most important meal of the day. It can also be the best! And in this chapter, you will see how wholesome brown rice plays a starring role in nutritious, delicious breakfast dishes that are light, easy to digest, and wonderfully satisfying—foods that can energize and keep you going for hours!

Is there anything better than a bowl of hot creamy porridge to warm you up on a cold winter morning? This chapter offers some delicious varieties, from the simple Japanese *Okayu* (the country's traditional brown rice breakfast dish) to others like heavenly Apple-Cinnamon Rice and Oat Porridge. All are warming and wonderful, and guaranteed to help you get your day off to a great start.

Brown rice, whether alone or in combination with other healthful grains, lends wholesome goodness to many other breakfast favorites. Be sure to try a stack of Brown Rice and Blueberry Pancakes topped with your favorite syrup, or the simple yet no less spectacular Brown Rice Waffles crowned with an array of fresh fruit. There is even a recipe for waffles made with *mochi*—a sweet brown rice cake. Called "moffles," these delectable waffles are steadily growing in popularity, and once you've tried them, I'm confident you'll understand why.

Whether it's sitting down to a bowl of wholesome Muesli, grabbing a Crispy Rice Breakfast Bar to eat on the run, or enjoying a mile-high stack of delectable Multi-Grain Pancakes at your leisure, the choices in this chapter are great ways to begin your day.

Apple-Cinnamon Rice & Oat Porridge

*Apples and cinnamon add a flavorful touch
to this comforting breakfast favorite.
Rolled oats give it added creaminess.*

1. Place all of the ingredients except the pecans in a heavy medium-size pot. Cover and bring to a boil over high heat.

2. Reduce the heat to medium-low. Cover and simmer, stirring occasionally, for 10 to 15 minutes or until the rice and oats are soft and creamy.

3. Spoon the porridge into individual bowls, garnish with pecans, and serve.

FOR A CHANGE . . .

● Substitute rolled rye, kamut, or spelt cereal flakes for the rolled oats.

● Instead of pecans, use roasted walnuts or almonds.

● Omit the nuts and use roasted sunflower, pumpkin, sesame seeds, or Gomashio (page 67).

● Add a drop or two of vanilla for extra flavor.

● Instead of apples, try dried fruits that don't need to be soaked before cooking. Dried cranberries, blueberries, raisins, currants, chopped apricots, and chopped cherries are all good choices.

Yield: 4 to 5 servings

2 cups cooked short- or
medium-grain brown rice
(page 19)

$^1/_2$ cup rolled oats

3 cups cold water or
vanilla soymilk

$^1/_3$ cup dried apples, soaked
and coarsely chopped

1 tablespoon maple syrup

$^1/_2$ teaspoon cinnamon

Coarsely chopped roasted
pecans for garnish

A Little Rice Trivia . . .

There are over 40,000 different varieties of rice.

Pumpkin Porridge

The pumpkin imparts a beautiful yellow-orange color to this porridge, while the spices give it a taste that's reminiscent of pumpkin pie.

1. Place the rice, water, pumpkin, and salt in a heavy medium-size pot. Cover and bring to a boil over high heat.

2. Reduce the heat to medium-low. Simmer, stirring occasionally, for 1 hour or until the rice is soft and creamy.

3. Remove the lid, reduce the heat to low, and add the vanilla, cinnamon, and nutmeg. Stir well and continue to simmer for 2 or 3 minutes.

4. Spoon the porridge into individual serving bowls. Garnish with nuts and drizzle with maple or brown rice syrup before serving.

FOR A CHANGE . . .

- Millet, brown rice, and pumpkin are a delicious combination. Try this recipe with $3/4$ cup brown rice and $1/4$ cup rinsed millet.

- Garnish with a sprinkling of Gomashio (page 67) instead of nuts.

- For a richer-tasting porridge with slightly higher protein, use half water and half vanilla soymilk.

Yield: 4 to 5 servings

1 cup short- or medium-grain brown rice, rinsed and drained

5 cups cold water

2 cups cubed Hokkaido pumpkin or buttercup squash

1 pinch sea salt

1 teaspoon vanilla

1 teaspoon cinnamon

$1/4$ teaspoon ground nutmeg

Coarsely chopped roasted walnuts or pecans for garnish

Okayu
Brown Rice Porridge

This traditional Japanese rice porridge is the country's most popular. Considered a breakfast favorite, okayu is customarily garnished with savory ingredients—gomashio (sesame salt condiment), toasted nori sea vegetable, and pickled umeboshi plum. The traditional Japanese recipe is below, but be sure to check the "For a change" entries for variations.

Yield: 4 to 5 servings

I cup short-grain brown rice, rinsed and drained

5 cups cold water

I pinch sea salt

I sheet toasted nori, cut into 2-inch squares or thin strips

I umeboshi plum, pitted and finely chopped

4 teaspoons Gomashio (page 67)

1. Place the rice, water, and salt in a heavy medium-size pot. Cover and bring to a boil over high heat.

2. Reduce the heat to medium-low and simmer, stirring occasionally, for 1 hour or until the rice is soft and tender.

3. Spoon the porridge into individual bowls and garnish with equal amounts of nori, umeboshi, and gomashio. Serve hot.

FOR A CHANGE . . .

• Substitute chopped roasted nuts for the gomashio.

• Instead of the savory garnishes used in the traditional recipe, toss in some dried fruit, such as raisins, cranberries, blueberries, or currants.

• Serve with a drizzle of maple syrup, brown rice syrup, or your favorite sweetener.

• Substitute $1/4$ cup of the brown rice with another grain, such as sweet brown rice, millet, barley, or quinoa.

Lickety Split Breakfast Sandwich

Brown rice cakes are great alternatives to toast. In this recipe, they are used to make a quick, nutritious breakfast sandwich.

1. Warm the rice cakes in a toaster or toaster oven for 1 to 2 minutes. Be careful not to burn.

2. Spread the nut butter on one rice cake, top with the banana slices, and then cover with the second rice cake. Enjoy like a sandwich.

Yield: 1 sandwich

2 brown rice cakes

1 tablespoon peanut, almond, or cashew butter

1 small banana, sliced into rounds

FOR A CHANGE . . .

● Instead of banana, spread fruit jam or fruit butter on top of the nut butter.

ABOUT RICE PORRIDGE

Rice porridge—of which there are countless variations—is traditional breakfast fare for millions of people throughout Asia. In China, it is called *jook* or *juk;* in India, *ganji;* and in Japan, *okayu. Congee* is a catchall term for any type of soft rice porridge.

While seasonings and ingredients may vary, all rice porridges have two things in common—rice and lots of water. The most basic variety is made using only these two ingredients, while others are more elaborate. Savory variations may include salt and other seasonings, vegetables, and even fish or seafood. For sweeter rice porridge, fresh or dried fruit, brown rice syrup, or maple syrup is typically added to the basic ingredients, while flavor enhancers like vanilla, cinnamon,

and nutmeg are common choices. Chopped nuts, which offer added taste, nutrition, and texture, are another popular addition.

Although it is often enjoyed for breakfast, rice porridge can be served at any meal. When simply prepared, it is usually accompanied by several side dishes. Heartier variations can serve as complete meals.

In most countries, refined white rice is commonly used to prepare porridge, but using brown rice makes the dish healthier and more nutritious. The usual proportion of rice to water is 1 part rice to 5 parts water; however, this ratio can vary depending on the desired thickness. Short- or medium-grain brown rice is recommended for creating the creamiest porridge.

Brown Rice and Blueberry Pancakes

Naturally sweet and moist, these delectable pancakes are great for using up leftover brown rice.

Yield: 8 to 10 pancakes (3–4 inches)

I cup cooked short-, medium-, or long-grain brown rice (page 19)

I cup unbleached white flour

$^1/_2$ cup whole wheat pastry flour

2 teaspoons baking powder

I pinch sea salt

1 $^1/_4$ cups Soy Buttermilk (page 72)*

$^1/_4$ cup water

2 tablespoons extra virgin olive oil

I cup fresh or frozen blueberries

* Instead of soy buttermilk, you can use 1 medium egg and 1 $^1/_4$ cups plain or vanilla soymilk.

1. Combine the rice, white flour, pastry flour, baking powder, and salt in a large mixing bowl. Set aside.

2. Place the soy buttermilk, water, and oil in a small bowl or measuring cup, and stir until well blended.

3. Add the soymilk mixture to the flour mixture and stir to form a thick batter. Fold in the blueberries.

4. Heat a nonstick pancake griddle over medium-high heat. (If the griddle is not nonstick, lightly coat with oil.)

5. Spoon the batter in $^1/_4$- to $^1/_3$-cup amounts onto the hot griddle and spread with the back of the spoon into 3- to 4-inch rounds. Cook 2 to 3 minutes or until browned on the bottom. Flip the pancakes over and brown the other side.

6. Serve hot with your favorite sweetener, fruit sauce, or other topping. Try the Blueberry-Peach Syrup (page 74) or Strawberry-Blueberry Syrup (page 75).

FOR A CHANGE . . .

- Add $^1/_4$ cup chopped walnuts or pecans to the batter for added crunch.
- For increased flavor, add $^1/_2$ teaspoon vanilla in Step 2.

Multi-Grain Pancakes

Using two different flours and two types of rice increases the nutritional value of these multi-grain pancakes, while adding flavor and texture. Any leftover cooked grain also works well in these breakfast favorites.

1. Combine the whole wheat flour, corn flour, brown rice, wild rice, baking powder, and salt in a large mixing bowl. Set aside.

2. Place the soy buttermilk, vanilla soymilk, and oil in a small bowl or measuring cup, and stir until well blended.

3. Add the soymilk mixture to the flour mixture and stir to form a thick batter.

4. Heat a nonstick pancake griddle over medium-high heat. (If the griddle is not nonstick, lightly coat with oil.)

5. Spoon the batter in $1/4$- to $1/3$-cup amounts onto the hot griddle and spread with the back of the spoon into 4- to 5-inch rounds. Cook 2 to 3 minutes or until browned on the bottom. Flip the pancakes over and brown the other side.

6. Serve hot with maple syrup, Strawberry-Blueberry Sauce (page 75), Lemon-Walnut Syrup (page 75), fresh berries, or your favorite topping.

Yield: 8 to 10 pancakes
(4–5 inches)

1 cup whole wheat flour

$1/2$ cup corn flour

$1/2$ cup cooked short-, medium-, or long-grain brown rice (page 19)

$1/2$ cup cooked wild rice

2 teaspoons baking powder

1 pinch sea salt

$1 1/4$ cups Soy Buttermilk (page 72)*

$1/4$ cup vanilla soymilk

2 tablespoons extra virgin olive oil

* Instead of soy buttermilk, you can use 1 medium egg and $1 1/4$ cups plain soymilk.

Rice is nice . . . for making music.

Fill two small plastic bottles halfway with raw rice, seal them tightly, and voila! You've just made a set of maracas!

Quick & Easy
Brown Rice Pancakes

When there is little time to make pancakes from scratch, simply add any cooked brown or wild rice to an organic commercial pancake mix. It's a fast and easy way to make pancakes that benefit from the extra fiber, flavor, and texture of brown rice.

1. Place the pancake mix, rice, soy buttermilk, and oil in a medium mixing bowl. Stir well to form a thick batter.

2. Heat a nonstick pancake griddle over medium-high heat. (If the griddle is not nonstick, lightly coat with sunflower or safflower oil.)

3. Spoon the batter in $1/4$- to $1/3$-cup amounts onto the hot griddle and spread with the back of the spoon into 3- to 4-inch rounds. Cook 2 to 3 minutes or until browned on the bottom. Flip the pancakes over and brown the other side.

4. Serve hot with maple syrup, Strawberry-Blueberry Sauce (page 75), Lemon-Walnut Syrup (page 75), or your favorite topping.

FOR A CHANGE . . .

- Add $1/4$ cup fresh blueberries or other berries to the batter.

Yield: 5 to 7 pancakes
(3–4 inches)

I cup organic multi-grain or buckwheat pancake mix

$1/2$ cup cooked short-, medium-, or long-grain brown rice
(page 19)

$3/4$ cup Soy Buttermilk (page 72)*

I tablespoon safflower or extra virgin olive oil

* Instead of soy buttermilk, you can use 1 medium egg and $1 1/4$ cups plain soymilk.

Rice is nice . . .
for amusing your cat.

Add a little raw rice to a clean empty pill vial, seal it tightly, and watch your cat bat around this new toy.

Brown Rice Waffles

*Brown rice gives these waffles added lightness,
sweetness, and nutrition. Delicious!*

1. Combine the rice, pastry flour, brown rice flour, baking powder, and salt in a medium mixing bowl, and set aside.

2. Place the soy buttermilk, oil, and water in a small bowl or measuring cup, and stir until well blended.

3. Add the soymilk mixture to the flour mixture and stir to form a thick batter.

4. Heat up a nonstick waffle iron. (If the iron is not nonstick, lightly coat with oil.)

5. Spoon $1/3$ cup batter onto the hot iron, and spread with the back of the spoon. Close the lid, and cook about 3 to 4 minutes or until the lid lifts easily and the waffle is golden brown.

6. Serve hot with Strawberry-Blueberry Sauce (page 75), Blueberry-Peach Syrup (page 74), maple syrup, or your favorite topping.

FOR A CHANGE . . .

- Use half brown rice and half wild rice or millet.
- For an even lighter waffle, substitute part of the brown rice with white rice.
- Instead of brown rice flour, try using corn, quinoa, or Kamut flour.
- Add fresh or frozen berries to the batter.
- Add unsweetened chocolate chips to the batter.

Yield: About 4 to 5 waffles

1 cup cooked short-, medium-, or long-grain brown rice (page 19)

1 cup whole wheat pastry flour

$1/2$ cup brown rice flour

2 teaspoons baking powder

$1/4$ teaspoon sea salt

$1 1/4$ cups Soy Buttermilk (page 72)*

2 tablespoons extra virgin olive oil

$1/2$ cup water

* Instead of soy buttermilk, you can use 1 medium egg and $1 1/4$ cups plain or vanilla soymilk.

Crispy Rice Breakfast Bars

A delicious mix of flavors and textures, these bars are a real family favorite. I usually make double batches and keep them refrigerated or frozen to always have some on hand. They are great as a quick breakfast food, dessert, or anytime snack.

**Yield: About 18 bars
(1$\frac{1}{2}$-x-4-inches)**

2 cups crisped brown rice cereal

$\frac{1}{4}$ cup raisins

$\frac{1}{4}$ cup roasted pumpkin seeds

$\frac{1}{4}$ cup roasted sunflower seeds

$\frac{1}{4}$ cup maple syrup

$\frac{1}{4}$ cup brown rice syrup*

* If you don't have brown rice syrup, increase the maple syrup to $\frac{1}{2}$ cup.

1. Lightly oil a 13-x-9-inch baking dish and set aside.

2. Combine the cereal, raisins, pumpkin seeds, and sunflower seeds in a medium mixing bowl. Set aside.

3. Place the maple syrup and brown rice syrup in a small saucepan and bring to a boil while stirring constantly. Reduce the heat to low, continue to stir, and simmer 5 to 7 minutes or until the syrup starts to thicken.

4. Pour the hot syrup over the cereal mixture and mix thoroughly.

5. Transfer the mixture to the prepared baking dish. With slightly moistened hands, press it down firmly into an even layer.

6. Refrigerate for 30 minutes or until the syrup completely cools and hardens.

7. Cut the hardened mixture into 1$\frac{1}{2}$-x-4-inch bars and serve. Store leftovers in a covered container in the pantry, refrigerator, or freezer.

FOR A CHANGE . . .

● Try using a combination of crisped and puffed whole grain cereal.

● Add $\frac{1}{2}$ teaspoon of cinnamon to the mixture in Step 1.

- Instead of or in addition to the seeds, use coarsely chopped roasted pecans, walnuts, hazelnuts, almonds, or peanuts.

- Try using other dried fruit in place of or in addition to the raisins.

- For a richer, caramel-like flavor, add $^1/_2$ teaspoon vanilla and 1 or 2 tablespoons of peanut butter to the syrup in Step 3.

Granola

Just about everyone loves granola. Sweet and crunchy, it makes a nutritious breakfast cereal, as well as a snack to enjoy at any time of the day.

1. Preheat the oven to 325°F.

2. Place the oil, maple syrup, honey, vanilla, cinnamon, and salt in a large mixing bowl and stir well. Add the cereal flakes and oats, and stir until well combined.

3. Spread out the mixture evenly on a large baking sheet. Bake for 30 to 35 minutes or until the mixture is crisp and dry. For even baking, turn the mixture with a spatula every 7 to 10 minutes as it bakes.

4. Transfer the mixture to a large bowl, add the dried fruit, nuts, and seeds, and mix thoroughly.

5. Cool completely before storing in an airtight container.

FOR A CHANGE . . .

- For different tasting granola, use other combinations of cereal flakes and sweeteners.

- Use different combinations of dried fruit, nuts, and seeds.

Yield: About 5 cups

$^1/_4$ cup safflower or sunflower oil

3 tablespoons maple syrup

3 tablespoons honey

1 teaspoon vanilla

$^1/_2$ teaspoon cinnamon

$^1/_4$ teaspoon sea salt

1 cup brown rice cereal flakes

1 cup Kamut, spelt, or rye cereal flakes

1 cup rolled oats

$^1/_2$ cup dried blueberries, cranberries, or raisins

$^1/_2$ cup chopped roasted walnuts, pecans, hazelnuts, or almonds

$^1/_4$ cup roasted pumpkin or sunflower seeds

Moffles
Mochi Waffles

When pieces of mochi are pan-fried, baked, or deep-fried, they puff up like marshmallows, becoming crunchy on the outside yet tender and somewhat chewy on the inside. This makes mochi, which is also gluten-free, a great choice for waffles, or "moffles" as they are sometimes called (mochi + waffles = moffles). They are easy to make, versatile, and as an added bonus, mochi won't stick to the waffle iron like flour batter.

Yield: 4 to 5 waffles

1 pound brown rice mochi

1. Heat up a waffle iron. While it is heating up, coarsely grate the mochi or cut it into thin $1/4$-inch strips.

2. Place about $1/3$ cup grated mochi (or a few strips) into each of the four sections of the hot waffle iron. Close the lid.

3. Cook for 3 to 5 minutes or until you can easily lift the lid. The waffle should be slightly crisp to the touch and golden brown in color.

4. Repeat with the remaining mochi.

5. Serve with Strawberry-Blueberry Sauce (page 75), Lemon-Walnut Syrup (page 75), fresh berries, maple syrup, or your favorite topping.

FOR A CHANGE . . .

● After adding the mochi to the waffle iron, toss in some fresh or frozen berries. They will melt into the mochi as it cooks.

● Use cinnamon-raisin mochi instead of plain.

● Along with enjoying these delicious waffles for breakfast, you can serve them as "anytime" snacks. Crown them with a generous spread of nut or fruit butter, or serve them alongside savory dips, sauces, or salsas.

Muesli

Created in Europe as the ideal breakfast, traditional muesli consists of rolled oats and/or mixed whole grain cereal flakes, fresh or dried fruit, and nuts and/or seeds. It is usually soaked a few minutes in water, apple juice, or milk to soften before serving. (I recommend soy, almond, oat, or rice milk.) If using fresh fruit, add it just before serving. Feel free to double or even triple this recipe!

1. Combine all of the ingredients and store in an airtight container in the pantry for two to three weeks, in the refrigerator for one or two months, or in the freezer up to six months.

2. To serve, place ¹/₂ cup muesli in a bowl, and add 1 cup water, apple juice, or nondairy milk—soy, rice, oat, or almond. (The amount of liquid may vary depending on the desired thickness.) Let sit about 5 to 10 minutes to soften before serving.

FOR A CHANGE . . .

- Use different combinations of whole grain cereal flakes and dried fruit.
- Omit dried fruit from the mixture and add fresh chopped apples, peaches, nectarines, and/or pears, as well as fresh whole berries to the flake mixture just before soaking.
- Add a generous dash of cinnamon, ground nutmeg, allspice, or a combination of these flavorings to individual portions before serving.
- Add a dash of vanilla just before serving.
- Soak the muesli overnight in the refrigerator, and enjoy cold for breakfast. (This is how it is customarily served in Europe.)

Yield: About 4 cups

1 cup brown rice cereal flakes

1 cup Kamut, rye, or spelt cereal flakes

1 cup rolled oats

¹/₄ cup raisins

¹/₄ cup dried cranberries or blueberries

¹/₄ cup coarsely chopped roasted hazelnuts, walnuts, or pecans

Corn Rice Muffins

*Corn muffins are considered a breakfast staple throughout the
United States, especially in the South. In this nutritious
variation, brown rice gives the muffins a touch
of sweetness and a light, moist texture.*

Yield: 12 muffins

I cup cornmeal or corn flour

I cup whole wheat pastry flour

1 1/2 cups cooked short-,
medium-, or long-grain brown rice
(page 19)

I tablespoon baking powder

1/2 teaspoon sea salt

I cup plain unsweetened soymilk

1/4 cup safflower oil

I tablespoon apple cider vinegar

1/4 cup maple syrup

1. Preheat the oven to 400°F. Lightly oil a standard 12-cup muffin tin and set aside.

2. Combine the cornmeal, pastry flour, rice, baking powder, and salt in a medium mixing bowl. Set aside.

3. Place the soymilk, oil, and vinegar in a small bowl and stir well. Let the mixture sit for 5 minutes or until curds form. Add the maple syrup and stir well.

4. Add the soymilk mixture to the flour mixture and stir until just blended. Do not overstir.

5. Spoon the batter into the prepared muffin tin, filling each cup about 3/4 full.

6. Bake for 15 to 20 minutes, or until a toothpick inserted into the center of a muffin comes out clean.

7. Remove from the oven. Let the muffins cool at least 10 minutes before removing from the tin. Serve warm or at room temperature.

FOR A CHANGE . . .

● Use unbleached white flour instead of pastry flour for added lightness.

● For added taste and texture, stir 1/3 cup of sweet corn into the batter.

3

Salads, Soups & Stews

One of my most vivid childhood memories is walking into our house and being greeted by the heady aroma of homemade soup as it slowly simmered on the stove. It was warm and comforting and always welcomed. Whenever I put up a pot of soup for my own family, I always hope it gives them that same warm feeling.

In this chapter, you'll find a nice selection of soups that spotlight brown rice, from light and brothy miso soups, to heartier choices like Wild Rice Mushroom Bisque and the savory Lentil Rice. Because I believe the best soups begin with a rich, flavorful stock, I have included recipes for three that I consider staples—vegetable, mushroom, and a Japanese favorite called *dashi*.

I use stock not only as a foundation for soup, but also as the basis for my stews. Among the choices in this chapter are the classic Hoppin' John—a Southern favorite that is traditionally eaten before noon on New Year's Day to bring luck in the coming year—as well as a stick-to-your-ribs Pinto Bean Stew that is as delicious as it is satisfying.

Also included in this chapter is a wide variety of delectable grain salads. Brown rice partners beautifully with other whole grains, beans, and vegetables in recipes like Wild Rice Salad and the Mediterranean Rice and Barley Salad. Beets and red quinoa give the Crimson Rice and Quinoa Salad its beautiful vibrant color. And when there's no time to cook, be sure to try the Fiesta Salad, made with leftover rice, black turtle beans, and a colorful array of vegetables.

Whether you're in the mood for a light lunch or a hearty dinner, you will find whatever suits your mood in this chapter. Enjoy!

Quick
Brown Rice Salad

Using leftovers is not only economical; it also makes for quick preparation. Combining both raw and stir-fried vegetables gives this salad a light, refreshing lift that is especially nice in the summer.

1. Place the rice and chickpeas in a large mixing bowl and set aside.

2. Heat the oil in a medium-size skillet over medium-low heat. Add the garlic and mushrooms, and sauté 2 to 3 minutes or until soft. Add to the rice mixture.

3. Add all of the remaining ingredients to the bowl and toss gently to mix. Serve as is or refrigerate and enjoy chilled.

Yield: 4 to 5 servings

4 cups cooked short-, medium-, or long-grain brown rice (page 19)

2 cups cooked chickpeas (rinse if canned)

2 tablespoons extra virgin olive oil

1 clove garlic, minced

1 cup sliced fresh shiitake or crimini mushrooms*

$1/2$ cup blanched julienned carrots

$1/2$ cup blanched cut green beans (1-inch pieces)

$1/2$ cup finely chopped scallions

2 tablespoons Gomashio (page 67), or 2 tablespoons toasted sesame seeds and $1/4$ teaspoon sea salt

2 tablespoons fresh lemon juice

1 teaspoon minced fresh basil

* If using shiitake, remove the stems.

A Little Rice Trivia . . .

❑ In India, rice is the first food a new bride gives her husband. It is also the first food offered to a newborn.

❑ In Japan, soaking rice before cooking is believed to release the grains' life energy, giving the eater a more peaceful soul.

Crimson Rice and Quinoa Salad

With the highest protein content of all grains, quinoa is a nutritional powerhouse that adds a light fluffy quality and slight crunch to brown rice dishes. It is available in red, white, and black varieties. You can use any color quinoa for this recipe, but I prefer the red because it adds to the dish's beautiful crimson color.

1. Place the rice, quinoa, beets, water, and salt in a heavy medium-size pot. Cover and bring to a boil over high heat.

2. Reduce the heat to medium-low, stir once, and cover. Simmer 45 to 50 minutes or until the liquid is absorbed and the grains are tender. Remove from the heat, let sit for 10 minutes, then transfer to a mixing bowl. Fluff with a fork and let cool to room temperature.

3. Add all of the remaining ingredients except the peas to the cooled rice mixture and toss well.

4. Spoon the mixture in the middle of a serving platter and surround with peas. Serve as is or refrigerate and enjoy chilled.

FOR A CHANGE . . .

- Substitute shelled edamame for the green peas.

Yield: 4 to 5 servings

1 cup long-grain brown or red rice, rinsed and drained

1 cup red quinoa, rinsed and drained

2 small beets, peeled and diced

3 1/2 cups cold water

1 pinch sea salt

1/3 cup thinly sliced or quartered red radishes

1/4 cup finely chopped red onion

1/4 cup finely chopped chives or scallions

1/4 cup dried cranberries

1/4 cup extra virgin olive oil

1 tablespoon umeboshi vinegar, or 1 tablespoon red wine vinegar plus 1/4 teaspoon sea salt

1 teaspoon lemon zest

1 1/2 cups blanched fresh or frozen green peas

Wild Rice Salad

*Umeboshi vinegar adds a delicious salty tang
to this flavorful wild rice salad.*

Yield: 4 to 5 servings

1 cup wild rice, rinsed and drained*

$^1/_2$ cup long-grain brown basmati
or red rice, rinsed and drained

2$^1/_2$ cups cold water

1 pinch sea salt

1$^1/_2$ cups blanched green beans
(1-inch pieces)

2 cups blanched fresh or frozen
sweet corn

$^1/_2$ cup blanched fresh or frozen
green peas

$^1/_2$ cup finely diced red onion

$^1/_2$ cup diced red bell pepper

$^1/_4$ cup finely diced celery

1 cup coarsely chopped
roasted pecans

$^1/_3$ cup dried cranberries

$^1/_4$ cup extra virgin olive oil

1$^1/_2$ tablespoons umeboshi vinegar,
or 1$^1/_2$ tablespoons apple cider
vinegar and $^1/_4$ teaspoon sea salt

2 tablespoons fresh lemon juice

* Native American hand-harvested wild
rice is preferred (see page 130).

1. Place the rice, water, and salt in a heavy medium-size pot. Cover and bring to a boil over high heat.

2. Reduce the heat to medium-low, stir once, and cover. Simmer the rice for 25 to 30 minutes or until the liquid is absorbed and the grains are tender. Remove from the heat, let sit for 10 minutes, then transfer to a mixing bowl. Fluff with a fork and let cool to room temperature.

3. Add all of the remaining ingredients to the cooled rice and toss well. Serve as is or refrigerate and enjoy chilled.

FOR A CHANGE . . .

● Substitute raisins, dried blueberries, currants, or coarsely chopped cherries for the cranberries.

● Instead of pecans, use roasted walnuts, hazelnuts, almonds, pine nuts, sunflower seeds, or pumpkin seeds.

● For a different flavor, add $^1/_2$ teaspoon sage or poultry seasoning.

A Little Rice Trivia . . .

❏ There are more than 29,000 grains of uncooked long-grain rice in a single pound.

❏ It takes anywhere from 2,000 to 5,000 tons of water to produce one ton of rice.

Mediterranean Rice and Barley Salad

This light, refreshing rice and barley salad offers a delightful mix of sweet and salty flavors with a bit of tang from the dressing.

1. Place the rice, barley, water, and sea salt in a heavy medium-size pot. Cover and bring to a boil over high heat.

2. Reduce the heat to medium-low, stir once, and cover. Simmer 45 to 50 minutes or until the liquid is absorbed and the grains are tender. Remove from the heat, let sit for 10 minutes, then transfer to a mixing bowl. Fluff with a fork and let cool to room temperature.

3. Add the olives, carrots, raisins, almonds, and scallions to the cooled grains. Mix well.

4. Add the dressing and toss until well combined.

5. Spoon an equal amount of the rice mixture on each lettuce leaf and serve.

FOR A CHANGE . . .

- Substitute quinoa or wild rice for the barley.
- Use lightly toasted pine nuts or sunflower seeds instead of almonds.
- Instead of raisins, use dried blueberries, cranberries, or currants.

Yield: 4 to 5 servings

1 cup long-grain brown rice, rinsed and drained

1 cup partially pearled barley, rinsed and drained

4 cups cold water

1 pinch sea salt

$1/3$ cup pitted and coarsely chopped Kalamata or black olives

$1/4$ cup coarsely grated carrots

$1/4$ cup raisins

$1/3$ cup toasted slivered almonds

$1/4$ cup finely chopped scallions

$1/2$ cup Mustard-Lemon Dressing (page 69)

4 to 5 large romaine, Boston bib, butter crunch, or red lettuce leaves

Salsa Salad

Light and fluffy, red quinoa adds a spark of color and slight crunch to this salad, while salsa adds refreshing zest.

Yield: 4 to 5 servings

1 cup long-grain brown rice, rinsed and drained

1 cup red quinoa, rinsed and drained

3 1/2 cups cold water

2 cups cooked chickpeas (rinse if canned)

1 medium cucumber, diced

1 medium yellow summer squash, diced

1/3 cup pitted and halved Kalamata or black olives

2 1/2 cups Spicy Salsa (page 63) or commercial variety

1. Place the rice, quinoa, and water in a heavy medium-size pot. Cover and bring to a boil over high heat.

2. Reduce the heat to medium-low, stir once, and cover. Simmer for 45 to 50 minutes or until the liquid is absorbed and the grains are tender. Remove from the heat, let sit for 10 minutes, then transfer to a mixing bowl. Fluff with a fork and let cool to room temperature.

3. Add the chickpeas, cucumber, squash, and olives to the cooled mixture. Toss well.

4. Add the salsa to the rice mixture and toss until well combined. Serve as is or refrigerate and enjoy chilled.

Bifun Noodle Salad

Typically enjoyed in salads and soups, bifun rice noodles are an Asian cuisine staple. They are gluten free and cook quickly— only two or three minutes in boiling water. You can even "cook" bifun noodles by soaking them in hot water for about ten minutes.

Yield: 4 to 5 servings

6 to 7 ounces brown rice bifun noodles

1 1/2 cups blanched shredded green cabbage

1/2 cup blanched julienned carrots

1/3 cup finely sliced scallions

2 tablespoons brown rice vinegar

2 tablespoons shoyu soy sauce

2 tablespoons mirin, or 1 tablespoon maple syrup

2 1/2 teaspoons toasted sesame oil

1/2 teaspoon hot pepper sesame oil or chili oil

1. Cook the noodles according to package directions. Rinse, drain well, and place in a medium mixing bowl.

2. Add all of the remaining ingredients to the noodles. Toss gently until well combined. Serve as is or refrigerate and enjoy chilled.

Brown Rice and Red Quinoa Salad

Red quinoa adds visual interest and a pleasant crunch to this delicious salad. A sprinkling of gomashio adds a touch of salt and a mild nutty flavor.

1. Place the rice, quinoa, water, and sea salt in a heavy medium-size pot. Cover and bring to a boil over high heat.

2. Reduce the heat to medium-low, stir once, and cover. Simmer for 45 to 50 minutes or until the liquid is absorbed and the grains are tender. Remove from the heat, let sit for 10 minutes, then transfer to a mixing bowl. Fluff with a fork and let cool to room temperature.

3. Add the edamame, carrots, and scallions to the cooled grains. Mix gently.

4. Heat the vinegar and mirin in a small saucepan until hot but not boiling. Pour over the grains and toss until well combined.

5. Serve as is or refrigerate and enjoy chilled. Sprinkle with gomashio before serving.

FOR A CHANGE . . .

- Substitute wild rice or millet for the quinoa.
- Try green peas instead of edamame.
- Substitute white sushi rice or Arborio for the brown rice. You will have to decrease the water to 3 cups, and simmer the rice and quinoa in Step 2 about 20 minutes or until the grains are tender.

Yield: 4 to 5 servings

$1 \frac{1}{2}$ cups short- or long-grain brown rice, rinsed and drained

$\frac{1}{2}$ cup red quinoa, rinsed and drained

4 cups cold water

1 pinch sea salt

$\frac{1}{2}$ cup blanched shelled edamame

$\frac{1}{4}$ cup blanched diced carrots

$\frac{1}{4}$ cup finely minced scallion

2 tablespoons brown rice vinegar

2 tablespoons mirin, or 1 tablespoon maple syrup

Gomashio (page 67) for garnish

Chirashi Zushi
Scattered Rice Salad

Sometimes described as "sushi in a bowl," this mixed or scattered rice salad is customarily served in Japan on birthdays, holidays, and other special occasions. It is traditionally made with seasoned sticky white rice that is topped with a colorful array of ingredients. This version uses half brown rice for added nutrition.

Yield: 4 to 5 servings

$^1/_3$ cup dried shiitake mushroom slices

I cup warm water for soaking shiitake

I cup short-grain brown rice, rinsed and drained

I cup white sushi rice or Arborio rice, rinsed and drained

$3^1/_4$ cups cold water

I pinch sea salt

I teaspoon shoyu soy sauce

I teaspoon maple syrup

$^1/_4$ cup brown rice vinegar

3 tablespoons mirin or brown rice syrup

TOPPINGS

I cup blanched shelled edamame

$^1/_3$ cup blanched julienned carrots

$^1/_3$ cup finely chopped pickled ginger

2 to 3 tablespoons toasted sesame seeds

I sheet toasted nori, torn or cut into small pieces.

1. Soak the shiitake in the cup of warm water for 10 minutes or until soft.

2. Place the brown rice, white rice, cold water, and salt in a heavy medium-size pot. Cover and bring to a boil over high heat.

3. Reduce the heat to medium-low, stir once, and cover. Simmer for 45 to 50 minutes or until the liquid is absorbed and the rice is tender.

4. While the rice is cooking, bring the soaked shiitake, soaking water, shoyu, and maple syrup to boil in a small saucepan over high heat. Reduce the heat to low, cover, and simmer 20 minutes. Drain the shiitake and set aside.

5. When the rice is tender, remove from the heat and let sit for 10 minutes. Transfer to a large mixing bowl, fluff with a fork, and let cool to room temperature.

6. Place the vinegar and mirin in a small saucepan over medium heat until hot but not boiling. Pour over the rice. To combine the rice and vinegar, cut through the mixture very gently with a bamboo rice paddle or wooden spoon until the rice is well coated. This gentle cutting motion will aerate the mixture and keep the grains separate. Do not stir or mix the rice, which will make it mushy and cause it to clump.

7. Spoon the seasoned rice into individual bowls, and top with shiitake, edamame, carrots, ginger, and sesame seeds. Garnish with a sprinkling of nori before serving.

FOR A CHANGE . . .

- Instead of a combination of brown and white rice, try this recipe using all brown rice or all white.
- Other suggested toppings include scrambled egg or slices of egg omelet; bonito flakes; and cooked shrimp, crab, lobster, or smoked fish.

Fiesta Salad

No time to cook? Try this spicy salad made with leftover rice, black turtle beans, and a colorful array of vegetables.

1. Place all of the ingredients in a large serving bowl and toss until well combined.

2. Serve as is or refrigerate and enjoy chilled.

FOR A CHANGE . . .

- Substitute pinto, kidney, small red beans, or black-eyed peas for the black beans.
- For a different flavor, used chopped fresh parsley instead of cilantro.
- Substitute 1 to 2 teaspoons prepared hot sauce for the cayenne pepper.

Yield: 4 to 5 servings

2 cups cooked short-, medium-, or long-grain brown rice (page 19)

1 medium red bell pepper, diced

1 medium green bell pepper, diced

1 cup blanched fresh or frozen sweet corn

1 cup cooked black beans (rinse if canned)

2 tablespoons chopped fresh cilantro

1 teaspoon ground cumin

$1/8$ teaspoon cayenne pepper, or to taste

$1/2$ cup Citrus Vinaigrette (page 69), or other prepared vinaigrette

Vegetable Stock

*Although this vegetable stock is simple and basic,
it is also quite flavorful. For additional preparation pointers,
see "Making Stock" below.*

Yield: 1 gallon

4 quarts (16 cups) cold water

3 to 4 medium onions,
coarsely chopped

4 medium carrots, coarsely chopped

1 small rutabaga or 2 medium
turnips, coarsely chopped

1 stalk celery, coarsely chopped

1 medium leek, halved lengthwise
and coarsely chopped*

Handful fresh parsley sprigs

* After halving the leek, be sure to
rinse it well to remove any soil.

1. Place all of the ingredients in a large pot, cover, and bring to a boil over high heat. Reduce the heat to medium-low and simmer for 30 to 40 minutes.

2. Pour the contents of the pot into a colander that has been set over a pot or large heatproof bowl. Discard the vegetables.

3. The stock is now ready to use. To store for later use, first allow the stock to cool to room temperature, then place in sealed containers. Refrigerate up to one week or freeze up to six months.

MAKING STOCK

Flavorful stocks are great foundations for soups and stews. They also add richness to rice dishes, vegetables, and other savory foods. Although prepared stocks are readily available in supermarkets and natural foods stores, I prefer to make my own. Not only are they easy to make, they're great for using up any leftover vegetables you may have on hand.

In this chapter, I've shared my recipes for three basic stocks—Mushroom (page 49), Vegetable (above), and a staple Japanese stock made with kombu sea vegetable called Dashi (page 50). I usually portion these flavorful broths into various sized containers and store them in the freezer. That way, I always have some on hand to use at a moment's notice.

When preparing vegetable stock, keep in mind that there is no single recipe. What goes into it will depend on what you have on hand—including "scraps"

Mushroom Stock

Dried mushrooms give this stock a delicious sweet yet savory flavor, which the Japanese refer to as "umami." It is healthy, low in fat, and very simple to make.

1. Place all of the ingredients in a medium pot, cover, and bring to a boil over high heat. Reduce the heat to medium-low and simmer for 20 to 30 minutes.

2. Remove the mushrooms and reserve for another use.

3. The stock is now ready to use. To store for later use, first allow the stock to cool to room temperature, then place in sealed containers. Refrigerate up to one week or freeze up to three months.

Yield: 1 quart

4 cups water

I cup dried whole shiitake, or combination of your favorite dried mushrooms

I pinch sea salt

like carrot heels, kale ribs, and even onion skins! Use my basic recipe as a starting point for experimenting with your own ingredient choices. Also be aware that strong-flavored vegetables such as celery and parsnips can overpower the other flavors in the stock, so use them in lesser amounts than milder or sweeter vegetables like onions and carrots. When using root vegetables like carrots, turnips, rutabaga, and parsnips, peeling isn't necessary, but be sure to scrub them well.

To further elevate the flavor of a basic vegetable stock, try adding dried mushrooms and various herbs and/or spices. And for added depth and richness, roast or sauté the vegetables before cooking them in the stock.

Not only are homemade stocks simple to prepare, they are also healthier and more flavorful than most commercial varieties. As an added bonus, they are less expensive. Be sure to give them a try! You'll be glad you did.

Dashi
Kombu Stock

Made with kombu sea vegetable, this stock is the basis for traditional Japanese soups—including the broth for noodle soups and miso soups. It is also a flavor enhancer for grain, bean, and vegetable dishes. Dashi is very simple to make. I usually double or even triple the following basic recipe, which I then portion out and store in the refrigerator or freezer.

Yield: 6 cups

6 cups cold water

6- to 8-inch piece kombu
sea vegetable

1. Place the water and kombu in a medium pot, cover, and bring to a boil over high heat. Reduce the heat to medium-low and simmer for 4 to 5 minutes.

2. Remove and discard the kombu.*

3. The stock is now ready to use. To store for later use, first allow the stock to cool to room temperature, then place in sealed containers. Refrigerate up to one week or freeze up to three months.

* You can also finely chop the kombu and add it to grain, bean, or vegetable soups and stews.

FOR A CHANGE . . .

● Simmer 6 whole dried shiitake or ¹/₂ cup slices with the kombu. After cooking and removing the kombu, cover the pot and continue simmering the shiitake for 15 to 20 minutes. Remove the shiitake and reserve for another use, or finely chop and return to the stock.

● For a slight smoky flavor, add ¹/₂ cup dried bonito flakes to the stock after removing the kombu. Simmer for 5 minutes, then pour the stock through a fine mesh strainer that is set over a pot or large heatproof bowl. Discard the flakes.

Japanese Noodle Soup

This traditional soup is commonly served in noodle bars throughout Japan. It is made with udon noodles, which are similar in shape and thickness to linguine. When there's little time to cook, this soup makes a satisfying meal.

1. Cook the udon according to package directions. Rinse, drain, and set aside.

2. Place the dashi in a medium pot and bring to boil over high heat. Reduce the heat to low, add the tofu and soy sauce, and simmer for 1 to 2 minutes or until the tofu is heated through.

3. Add the udon to individual serving bowls. Ladle hot broth over the noodles, and top each serving with an equal portion of spinach, cabbage, and scallions.

FOR A CHANGE . . .

- Instead of or in addition to spinach and cabbage, top with sautéed vegetables.
- Sprinkle with toasted sesame seeds for extra flavor.
- Substitute cooked bifun noodles for udon.
- Season with miso instead of soy sauce.

Yield: 4 to 5 servings

8 ounces brown rice
udon noodles

6 cups Dashi (page 50) or Vegetable
Stock (page 48)

2 tablespoons shoyu soy sauce,
or to taste

1 cup cubed tofu

2 cups blanched spinach

1 cup blanched shredded
Chinese cabbage

Finely chopped scallions
for garnish

Rice is nice . . .
to keep salt from clumping.

When it's humid, even the smallest amount of moisture can cause sea salt to clump, making it nearly impossible to sprinkle from the shaker. To prevent this, add a few grains of raw rice to the shaker. The rice will absorb the moisture and keep the salt flowing freely.

Wild Rice Mushroom Bisque

This rich and creamy soup is a real winner,
and guaranteed to get rave reviews!

Yield: 5 to 6 servings

6 cups Mushroom Stock (page 49)
or commercial variety

1 cup brown rice flakes, or any
variety cooked brown rice

1 tablespoon extra virgin olive oil

1 cup sliced crimini mushrooms

1/2 cup sliced button mushrooms

2/3 cup wild rice, rinsed
and drained*

1 cup minced shallots

2 teaspoons finely chopped
fresh thyme

1 teaspoon sea salt, or to taste

1/4 teaspoon black pepper,
or to taste

2 cups plain unsweetened soymilk

2 tablespoons unbleached
white flour

Finely chopped fresh chives
for garnish

* Native American hand-harvested wild
rice is preferred (see page 130).

1. Bring the stock to boil in a medium pot over high heat. Reduce the heat to medium-low, add the brown rice flakes, and simmer for 5 minutes. Remove from the heat.

2. Transfer half the stock to a blender, and process several seconds or until the stock and flakes are well blended. Repeat with the remaining stock. Set aside.

3. Heat the oil in a heavy medium-size pot over medium-low heat. Add the mushrooms and sauté for 3 to 4 minutes or until they begin to soften.

4. Add the blended stock, wild rice, shallots, and thyme to the pot. Cover and bring to a boil over high heat. Reduce the heat to medium-low and simmer 20 to 25 minutes until the rice is tender.

5. Add the salt and pepper, then reduce the heat to low.

6. Whisk together the soymilk and flour to form a smooth paste. Add the paste to the pot, then stir constantly for 4 to 5 minutes or until the soup begins to thicken. Do not allow the soup to boil or the soymilk will curdle.

7. Spoon the soup into individual serving bowls, garnish with chives, and serve.

FOR A CHANGE . . .

• For a touch of sweetness, add 1 tablespoon maple syrup in Step 5.

• Although not preferred, use water instead of stock.

• Use any mushroom variety or combination of different types. If using dried, first soak them in warm water for 20 minutes. Use the soaking water as part of the stock measurement.

Lentil Rice Soup

When complemented with a simple green salad and some whole grain bread, this hearty soup makes a delicious and satisfying main meal.

1. Heat the oil in a heavy medium-size pot over medium-low heat. Add the garlic and onion, and sauté for 3 to 5 minutes or until they begin to soften.

2. Add the stock, rice, lentils, carrots, celery, bay leaves, and red pepper flakes to the pot. Cover and bring to a boil over high heat. Reduce the heat to medium-low and simmer for 25 to 30 minutes.

3. Add the tomatoes, salt, and pepper. Continue to simmer another 15 to 20 minutes or until the rice is tender.

4. Stir the spinach, parsley, and zest into the soup, and simmer 3 to 4 minutes. Remove and discard the bay leaves.

5. Spoon the piping hot soup into bowls and serve.

FOR A CHANGE . . .

• Try using wild rice instead of brown. Reduce the simmering time in Step 2 to about 15 minutes.

• Before serving, top with a spoonful of Tofu Sour Cream (page 74).

• Although not preferred, you can use water instead of vegetable stock.

Yield: 5 to 6 servings

2 tablespoons extra virgin olive oil

2 cloves garlic, minced

$1/2$ cup diced onion

5 cups Vegetable Stock (page 48) or commercial variety

$1/2$ cup short-, medium-, or long-grain brown rice, rinsed and drained

15-ounce can lentils, not drained

$1/4$ cup diced carrots

$1/4$ cup diced celery

2 bay leaves

1 pinch crushed red pepper flakes

1 cup canned whole tomatoes, coarsely chopped

1 teaspoon sea salt

$1/4$ teaspoon black pepper

1 cup chopped spinach or Swiss chard

$1/4$ cup minced fresh parsley

$1/4$ teaspoon lemon zest

French Onion Soup with Mochi

This French onion soup is one of my all-time favorites. Its luscious rich flavor comes from just a few simple ingredients—sweet onions, nutty sesame oil, earthy mushrooms, and smoky bonito flakes. Unlike traditional French onion soup, which is topped with Gruyère or other type of Swiss cheese, this healthier, lower-fat version uses grated brown rice mochi, which melts like cheese over the hot soup.

Yield: 4 to 6 servings

2 teaspoons toasted or plain sesame oil

5 cups thinly sliced Spanish or Vidalia onions

5 cups Vegetable Stock (page 48) or commercial variety

1 cup dried shiitake mushroom slices

¹/₄ cup bonito flakes

1 tablespoon shoyu soy sauce, or to taste

¹/₄ teaspoon sea salt

1 cup whole wheat croutons

¹/₂ cup coarsely grated brown rice mochi

Finely sliced scallions for garnish

1. Heat the oil in a medium pot over medium-low heat. Add the onions and sauté for 5 to 7 minutes or until soft and translucent.

2. Add the stock, shiitake, and bonito flakes to the pot. Cover and bring to a boil over high heat. Reduce the heat to medium-low and simmer for 25 to 30 minutes.

3. Add the shoyu and salt, reduce the heat to low, and simmer another 5 minutes.

4. Ladle the soup into individual ovenproof bowls. Top with croutons and grated mochi.

5. Place the bowls in a preheated 450°F oven. (I recommend putting the bowls on a cookie/baking sheet to prevent them from tipping over in the oven.) Bake for 8 to 10 minutes or until the mochi melts.

6. Garnish with scallions and serve piping hot.

FOR A CHANGE . . .

- Use any type or combination of dried mushrooms.
- Instead of scallions, garnish with chopped fresh parsley.

Miso Soup with Udon Noodles

Traditional miso soup—a popular breakfast choice in Japan—is brothy and simple, often served with nothing more than a garnish of chopped scallions. My heartier version, which can be enjoyed at any time of the day, contains mushrooms, tofu, spinach, and udon noodles, but feel free to add whatever ingredients you like. Root vegetables, seafood, leafy greens, and pieces of mochi are other popular choices.

1. Place the shiitake and water in a medium pot. Cover and bring to a boil over high heat. Reduce the heat to medium-low and simmer for 8 to 10 minutes.

2. While the shiitake are simmering, cook the udon noodles according to package directions. Rinse, drain, and set aside.

3. Place the miso and warm water in a small bowl and stir to form a smooth paste. Reduce the heat to low under the simmering stock, add the miso, spinach, tofu, and wakame. Simmer uncovered for 2 to 3 minutes.

4. Place equal amounts of noodles in individual soup bowls. Ladle the soup into the bowls, garnish with scallions, and serve.

FOR A CHANGE . . .

- Use bifun rice noodles instead of udon.
- Use any type or combination of dried mushrooms.
- Try a different miso variety or a combination of two or three types.
- For a smoky flavor, add $1/4$ cup bonito flakes in Step 1.

Yield: 4 to 5 servings

$1/2$ cup dried shiitake mushroom slices

4 cups water

8 ounces brown rice udon noodles

2 tablespoons brown rice (genmai) miso

3 tablespoons warm water

1 cup chopped fresh spinach

$1/2$ cup small cubes fresh tofu

1 tablespoon wakame flakes

Thinly sliced scallions for garnish

Miso Soup with Mochi

Adding brown rice mochi is a great way to incorporate whole grain goodness into this simple, single-serving soup.

Yield: 1 serving

2-x-3-inch piece brown rice mochi, quartered

1 cup water

1 teaspoon wakame flakes

1 tablespoon white rice (shiro) miso

2 tablespoons warm water

Sliced scallions for garnish

1. Arrange the mochi pieces on a baking tin and place in a 350°F oven (or toaster oven) for 5 to 7 minutes or until they puff up like marshmallows and becomes slightly brown. Remove and set aside.

2. While the mochi is baking, place the wakame and 1 cup water in a small pot and bring to a boil over high heat.

3. Place the miso and warm water in a small bowl and stir to form a smooth paste. Reduce the heat under the pot to low, add the miso, and simmer for 1 to 2 minutes.

4. Place the mochi pieces in an individual soup bowl and cover with the hot soup. Garnish with scallions and enjoy!

FOR A CHANGE . . .

● For a slight smoky flavor, add 1 teaspoon bonito flakes in Step 2.

● Instead of mochi, use about 1 cup cooked brown rice in Step 4.

● For added texture, add a few cubes of fresh tofu.

● Use a different variety of miso.

COOKING WITH MISO

A culinary staple in Japan, miso is a fermented soybean paste that is traditionally used to season soups, stews, dressings, and marinades. Miso is available in a variety of flavors, which depend on the grain or bean it contains, as well as the length of fermentation.

Typical Japanese misos are made exclusively from soybeans, usually with the addition of cultured rice or barley; however, today, you can find varieties made with ingredients like chickpeas and millet. Lighter-colored misos are mild flavored and commonly used in light soups and cream-style sauces. Darker misos are stronger, saltier, and more robust, making them better choices for hearty soups, stews, and savory dishes.

Along with its role as a flavor enhancer, miso is considered a "super food" among health care professionals. It contains enzymes that help aid digestion, as well as essential fatty acids and soy isoflavones that are effective in preventing and treating a number of health conditions, including osteoporosis, heart disease, hypertension, and certain cancers. In order to maximize miso's beneficial health properties, it should not be boiled. Rather, it should be added to the dish at the end of cooking time.

When buying miso, be aware that most commercial varieties are made with genetically modified soybeans. They are also artificially fermented, and may contain monosodium glutamate (MSG). For this reason, always look for traditionally fermented organic varieties.

BLANCHING VEGETABLES

Blanching is an easy, effective technique for keeping fresh vegetables crisp yet tender. It also helps them retain their color. Basically, the vegetables are boiled briefly, then rinsed under cold water (or plunged into an ice bath), which stops the cooking process and sets the color. When blanching vegetables, follow these easy steps:

1. Bring a pot of water to boil. (Adding salt to the water is optional.)

2. Add the vegetables to the pot and boil for 1 to 3 minutes, or until slightly cooked and firm yet tender. The color of the vegetables will tend to be bright in color at this point. (Blanching time will vary depending on the thickness and/or type of vegetable.) To test, remove one with a slotted spoon, run under cold water, and eat—it should be firm and nearly tender.

3. As soon as the vegetables are blanched, remove them from the pot. Either run them under cold water or plunge them into a bowl filled with water and ice cubes.

4. When the vegetables are no longer warm, drain them well.

5. Enjoy the blanched vegetables as they are, or use them according to specific recipe instructions.

Hoppin' John

This classic Southern stew is traditionally eaten before noon on New Year's Day to bring good luck in the coming year. It is referred to in the old saying, "Rice for riches, peas for peace." Usually made with white rice and pork, this version uses whole grain brown rice and seitan, which is available in most natural foods stores.

Yield: 5 to 6 servings

2 tablespoons extra virgin olive oil

1 cup chopped seitan

1 clove garlic, minced

1 $^1/_2$ cups diced onions

$^1/_4$ cup diced celery

4 cups Vegetable Stock (page 48) or commercial variety

2 cups cooked short-grain or brown basmati rice (page 19)

2 cans (15 ounces each) black-eyed peas, not drained

$^1/_2$ teaspoon sea salt

$^1/_4$ teaspoon black pepper

1 pinch crushed red pepper flakes, or to taste

2 cups chopped kale

Minced fresh parsley for garnish

Hot sauce for garnish

1. Heat the oil in a medium pot over medium-low heat. Add the seitan, sauté about 2 minutes, then add the garlic, onions, and celery. Continue to sauté another 2 to 3 minutes, or until the onions and celery begin to soften.

2. Add the stock, rice, black-eyed peas, salt, pepper, and pepper flakes to the pot. Cover and bring to a boil over high heat. Reduce the heat to medium-low, and simmer for 20 to 25 minutes.

3. Stir the kale into the pot, and simmer 5 to 7 minutes or until tender.

4. Spoon the piping hot stew into individual serving bowls. Enjoy as is or garnished with a sprinkle of parsley and a dash of hot sauce.

FOR A CHANGE . . .

● Substitute deep-fried tofu or tempeh cubes for the seitan.

● Instead of kale, use collards, chard, or spinach.

● For a tomato-flavored stew, add $^1/_4$ cup tomato paste or $^1/_2$ cup tomato sauce in Step 2.

● Although not preferred, you can use water instead of vegetable stock.

Brown Rice and Pinto Bean Stew

Warm and hearty, this stew is a perfect cold-weather meal. My family finds it even better reheated the next day.

1. Heat the oil in a medium pot over medium-low heat. Add the onion and garlic, and sauté for 2 to 3 minutes or until they begin to soften.

2. Add the stock, beans, and salt to the pot. Cover and bring to a boil over high heat. Reduce the heat to medium-low, and simmer for 15 minutes.

3. Add the tomatoes, bell pepper, corn, cumin, and chili powder. Reduce the heat to low, and continue to simmer another 15 minutes.

4. Stir the rice and parsley into the stew, and simmer another 5 minutes.

5. Spoon the piping hot stew into bowls and serve.

FOR A CHANGE . . .

- Instead of pinto beans, use kidney, navy, or Great Northern beans.
- For a different taste, use 2 teaspoons dried marjoram in place of the chili powder and cumin.

Yield: 5 to 6 servings

1 tablespoon extra virgin olive oil

1 medium onion, diced

2 cloves garlic, minced

4 cups Vegetable Stock (page 48) or commercial variety

2 cans (15 ounces each) pinto beans, not drained

1 teaspoon sea salt

2 medium tomatoes, chopped

$\frac{1}{2}$ cup diced green, red, or orange bell pepper

$\frac{1}{2}$ cup fresh or frozen sweet corn

1 teaspoon ground cumin

$\frac{1}{2}$ teaspoon chili powder, or to taste

3 cups cooked long-grain brown rice (page 19)

2 tablespoons chopped fresh parsley

A Little Rice Trivia . . .

In an effort to persuade children to eat all of their rice, Japanese parents playfully call the grains "Little Buddhas."

Yield: 4 to 5 servings

$^1/_2$ cup unbleached white or
whole wheat pastry flour

$^1/_2$ cup safflower oil or
extra virgin olive oil

1 cup diced onion

1 clove garlic, minced

4 cups Vegetable Stock (page 48)
or commercial variety

28-ounce can whole tomatoes,
coarsely chopped, not drained

2 cups cut fresh green beans
(1-inch pieces)

1 cup chopped okra

1 cup diced celery

$^1/_2$ cup diced green bell pepper

$^1/_2$ cup jarred roasted red peppers

$^1/_2$ cup diced carrots

$^1/_4$ cup diced parsnips

1 tablespoon ground cumin

1 teaspoon paprika

1 teaspoon dried oregano

$^1/_4$ teaspoon cayenne pepper,
or to taste

$^1/_2$ teaspoon sea salt

$^1/_8$ teaspoon black pepper

5 to 6 cups cooked long-grain
brown rice (page 19)

Vegetarian Gumbo over Brown Rice

This classic Southern-style vegetable stew is perfect over a bed of brown rice. It's made with roux—a mixture of equal parts flour and butter that is commonly used to thicken sauces and stews. I prefer using safflower or extra virgin olive oil instead of butter.

1. To make the roux, place the flour and oil in a heavy medium-size pot, and whisk until smooth. While constantly stirring, cook the mixture over medium heat for 15 to 20 minutes or until it becomes a rich reddish-brown.

2. Add all of the remaining ingredients except the rice to the pot and stir well. Cover and bring to a boil over high heat. Reduce the heat to medium-low. Stirring often, simmer for 35 to 40 minutes or until the vegetables are tender and the liquid is thick and creamy.

3. Adjust the seasonings and simmer another 5 minutes.

4. Spoon the rice into individual serving bowls, top with gumbo, and serve.

FOR A CHANGE . . .

- For extra protein, add a 15-ounce can of red beans or black-eyed peas to the pot as the ingredients simmer (Step 2).
- Add a dash of hot sauce for an extra fiery kick.
- Add 1 cup of cooked shellfish (shrimp, crab, crayfish, lobster, etc.) near the end of cooking time.
- Although not preferred, you can use water instead of vegetable stock.

4

Condiments, Toppings & Accompaniments

There certainly is truth to the old saying, "variety is the spice of life." And when it comes to food, adding the right sauce, topping, or flavorful condiment can elevate a favorite dish to spectacular new heights.

This chapter is dedicated to keeping mealtime boredom at bay by offering a number of incredible sauces, dressings, and other accompaniments to enhance the already delicious dishes found in this book. And what a great range of choices there are—hot and cold, savory and sweet.

You'll find a number of Asian-inspired dipping sauces that pair perfectly with the sushi rolls, samosas, and many other appetizing snacks found in Chapter 5. Along with the tangy Shoyu-Ginger Sauce, a rich Tahini-Lemon Sauce is recommended for adding a bit of zing to hearty stir-fries. Spicy Salsa gives South-of-the-Border choices like Mexican burritos and enchiladas a fiery kick, while fruity Pineapple Salsa adds welcomed sweetness to fried foods like brown rice fritters and crispy croquettes. There are also luscious syrups to drizzle over pancakes, zesty vinaigrettes to sprinkle on salads, and savory gravies to crown simple rice side dishes. There is even a recipe for gomashio—a centuries-old Japanese condiment that adds a salty, nutty flavor to dishes without adding as much sodium as regular table salt.

In addition to enhancing taste and enlivening dishes, you'll discover that the choices on the following pages contribute color, texture, and nutrients. Most are quick and easy to make, and, as an added bonus, they keep well. I often make one or two in advance to have on hand and use throughout the week.

Wasabi-Shoyu Dipping Sauce

Yield: About ²/₃ cup

2 tablespoons wasabi powder

2 to 3 teaspoons hot water

¹/₂ cup cold water

¹/₄ cup shoyu soy sauce

This flavorful sauce blends the saltiness of soy sauce with a fiery burst of wasabi. It partners perfectly with sushi rolls, and makes a great dip for Crispy Rice Noodles (page 85), Rice and Buckwheat Croquettes (page 79), and other fried foods.

1. Place the wasabi powder in a small bowl, add the hot water, and stir to form a thick paste.

2. Add the cold water and shoyu, and stir until well blended.

3. Use immediately, or store in an airtight container and refrigerate up to one week.

Shoyu-Ginger Sauce

The spicy ginger in this popular Asian-style sauce helps aid digestion, making it a popular choice to serve with fried foods, like the Golden Rice & Millet Nuggets on page 84. My family also sprinkles it over grain and bean burgers, and enjoys it as a dipping sauce for sushi rolls.

Yield: About ²/₃ cup

3 tablespoons finely grated fresh ginger

¹/₂ cup water

2 tablespoons shoyu soy sauce, or to taste

1. With your hands, squeeze the juice from the grated ginger into a small bowl. Add water and soy sauce, and stir until well blended.

2. Use immediately or store in an airtight container and refrigerate up to one week.

FOR A CHANGE . . .

● For a sweeter flavor, add 1 to 2 teaspoons mirin, rice cooking wine, pineapple juice, or honey.

Spicy Salsa

This salsa lends a spicy South-of-the-Border kick to lots of Mexican-inspired dishes. Be sure to try it with the Brown Rice and Bean Burritos (page 153), Rice 'n Bean Enchiladas (page 152), and Mexican Black Beans and Rice (page 122). Also a great topper for brown rice crackers and rice cakes.

1. Place all of the ingredients in a medium mixing bowl and stir well.

2. Use immediately or store in an airtight container and refrigerate up to one week.

FOR A CHANGE . . .

● To increase the heat, add 1 additional teaspoon of minced jalapeño, a dash or 2 of cayenne pepper, or a few drops of hot sauce.

Yield: About 4 cups

2 cups diced plum tomatoes

1 cup finely chopped red onion

$^1/_2$ cup finely chopped fresh parsley

2 cloves garlic, finely minced

$^1/_4$ cup orange juice

2 tablespoons red wine vinegar

1 teaspoon minced jalapeño pepper, or to taste

$^1/_2$ teaspoon ground cumin

$^1/_4$ teaspoon ground coriander

$^1/_4$ teaspoon sea salt

$^1/_8$ teaspoon black pepper

Pineapple Salsa

This zesty sweet salsa goes especially well with fried foods like Brown Rice and Corn Fritters (page 78), Rice and Buckwheat Croquettes (page 79), and Quick 'n Easy Samosas (page 80). It's also a tasty addition to Brown Rice and Bean Burritos (page 153).

1. Place all of the ingredients in a medium mixing bowl and stir well.

2. Refrigerate at least 1 hour before serving to let the flavors meld. Store leftovers in a tightly sealed container in the refrigerator up to one week.

Yield: About 2 cups

1$^1/_2$ cups chopped fresh pineapple

$^1/_4$ cup finely chopped red onion

$^1/_4$ cup finely chopped red bell pepper

2 tablespoons minced fresh cilantro or parsley

2 tablespoons fresh lime juice

1 teaspoon minced jalapeño or other hot chili pepper

1 small clove garlic, finely minced

1 pinch sea salt

Sweet and Sour Sauce

*An Asian staple, sweet and sour sauce adds a fresh burst of flavor
to any simple brown rice or noodle dish. It also makes a wonderful
dip for fried foods like Rice and Buckwheat Croquettes (page 79)
and Crispy Rice Noodles (page 85). Sweet and sour sauce has
many delicious variations. This is one of my favorites.*

Yield: About 2½ cups

1 cup Mushroom Stock (page 49),
Vegetable Stock (page 48), or water

1 cup unsweetened pineapple juice

¼ cup brown rice vinegar

2 tablespoons maple syrup or honey

2 tablespoons kuzu root starch

3 tablespoons cold water

1. Place the stock, pineapple juice, vinegar, and maple
syrup in a small saucepan over medium heat. Stir well and
heat until just beginning to boil.

2. Dissolve the kuzu in the cold water, and add to the pan.
Stir constantly for 1 or 2 minutes or until the sauce thickens.

3. The sauce is now ready to season with shoyu or sea
salt, and use hot, warm, or at room temperature. Store in
an airtight container and refrigerate up to five days. Reheat
before using.

FOR A CHANGE . . .

● Substitute apple juice for the pineapple juice.

● Squeeze the juice from 1 tablespoon grated ginger into the
thickened sauce.

● Add a dash or 2 of chili pepper, cayenne, or crushed red
pepper flakes for a spicy variation.

● For added texture and flavor, add ½ cup finely chopped
pineapple to the thickened sauce.

A Little Rice Trivia . . .

Japanese rice wine or sake (*sah-kay*) is the oldest known
alcoholic beverage. First produced in China around 4800 BC, sake
gained popularity in Japan, where generations-old family craftsmen
still produce high-quality premium versions. Westerners often
drink sake warm, but traditionally, it is served slightly chilled.

Honey-Mustard Sauce

Although there are many commercial versions of honey-mustard, making your own is certainly easy enough. Be sure to try this versatile sauce with Rice & Bean Burgers (page 156), Quick 'n Easy Samosas (page 80), and pan-fried Azuki Rice Balls (page 88).

1. Place all of the ingredients in a small saucepan over medium-high heat. Stirring constantly, bring the mixture nearly to a boil, then remove from the heat.

2. Use immediately or store in an airtight container and refrigerate up to one week. Best if served warm.

FOR A CHANGE . . .

- For added flavor, include 1 tablespoon smooth peanut butter to the ingredients.

Yield: About ½ cup

¼ cup water

2 tablespoons honey

2 tablespoons brown or yellow mustard

1 tablespoon minced fresh chives

⅛ teaspoon sea salt, or 1 teaspoon shoyu soy sauce

Roasted Red Pepper Sauce

Whenever I make Brown Rice and Corn Fritters (page 78), this is my "go-to" topping. This sauce is also delicious over Almond Rice (page 111), Mock Mashed Potatoes (page 106), and just about any rice and bean combination.

1. Place all of the ingredients in a blender and pulse to the desired consistency. For a chunky sauce, stir the ingredients in a bowl—do not mix in a blender.

2. Use immediately or store in an airtight container and refrigerate up to one week, or freeze up to three months.

Yield: About 2 cups

12-ounce jar roasted red peppers, drained and chopped

1 clove garlic, minced

3 tablespoons chopped fresh parsley, basil, or chives

1 tablespoon extra virgin olive oil

1 teaspoon balsamic vinegar

⅓ cup Vegetable Stock (page 48) or commercial variety

1 pinch sea salt

1 pinch black pepper

Sushi Furikake

Furikake (foo-ray-KAH-kay) is a type of Japanese low-sodium condiment often used at the table to flavor food. It has endless variations. This recipe is for a popular variety that is well-suited to flavor Japanese rice balls and sushi rolls.

Yield: About 1½ cups

½ cup tan sesame seeds, rinsed and drained

½ cup black sesame seeds, rinsed and drained

⅓ cup Ao (green) nori flakes*

2 tablespoons shiso condiment

* If unavailable, tear 1 sheet of toasted nori into small pieces, place in a blender, and pulse into a coarse powder.

1. Dry-roast the tan and black sesame seeds separately. (The black seeds contain less oil and roast faster than the tan.) Place the rinsed tan sesame seeds in a medium skillet over medium-high heat. Stir constantly until they start to pop. Reduce the heat to low and continue stirring until the seeds are light brown and emit a nutty aroma. Be careful not to burn.* Remove from the heat and set aside to cool.

2. Next, dry-roast the black sesame seeds, keeping in mind that they roast more quickly than the tan. Set aside to cool.

3. Place the cooled sesame seeds in an airtight container. Add the nori flakes and shiso, seal, and shake well.

4. Store in the pantry, where it will keep for about a month.

* To test for doneness, periodically take a tablespoon of the seeds as they roast, then drop them back into the skillet. When the seeds are completely roasted, they will easily fall off the spoon without sticking—an indication that all the water has evaporated and the seeds are sufficiently popped.

A Little Rice Trivia . . .

In many Asian cultures, rice symbolizes prosperity and fertility, which is how the age-old custom of tossing rice at newlyweds after the wedding ceremony originated. Recently, it was discovered that the rice was damaging to the birds that ate it off the ground, so the tradition is no longer practiced.

Gomashio

A centuries-old Japanese condiment of lightly dry-roasted sesame seeds and a little sea salt, gomashio is a staple in my home. Just a sprinkling adds nutty, slightly salty flavor to food without adding as much sodium as regular table salt. Try it on pilafs and other rice dishes, as well as soups, salads, and vegetables. Although gomashio is available in most natural foods stores, it is also very easy to make.

1. Place the salt in a small skillet over medium-high heat. Stir constantly for several seconds until it turns off white, and then transfer to a blender, and grind briefly to a powdery consistency. Leave in the blender.

2. Add the rinsed seeds to a medium skillet over medium-high heat. Stir constantly until they start to pop. Reduce the heat to low and continue stirring until the seeds are light brown and emit a nutty aroma. Be careful not to burn.*

3. Quickly transfer the seeds to the blender and grind briefly with the salt (it should be a little coarse with the seeds half crushed).

4. To store, allow the mixture to cool completely, and then place in a sealed container. Keep in the pantry, where it will keep for about a month.

* To test for doneness, periodically take a tablespoon of the seeds as they roast, then drop them back into the skillet. When the seeds are completely roasted, they will easily fall off the spoon without sticking—an indication that all the water has evaporated and the seeds are sufficiently popped. This surefire method of testing for doneness never fails to produce the most delicious gomashio.

Yield: About ¾ cup

2 teaspoons sea salt

I cup sesame seeds, rinsed and drained*

* Rinsed seeds roast more evenly than dried, and result in a more intense sesame flavor.

Peanut-Mustard Sauce

The rich nutty flavor of this tangy dipping sauce goes especially well with Asian-inspired brown rice dishes. Try it with Golden Rice & Millet Nuggets (page 84) or Quick 'n Easy Samosas (page 80). It also makes a great topper for Rice & Bean Burgers (page 156).

Yield: About ¾ cup

¼ cup smooth unsalted peanut butter

½ cup water

1½ tablespoons brown or yellow mustard

1 tablespoon honey or maple syrup

2 teaspoons shoyu soy sauce

1. Place all of the ingredients in a small saucepan over medium-high heat. Stirring constantly, bring the mixture nearly to a boil, then remove from the heat.

2. Use immediately or store in an airtight container and refrigerate up to one week. Reheat before using. (You may need to add a tablespoon or two of water when reheating as the sauce becomes quite thick when refrigerated.)

FOR A CHANGE . . .

- For added flavor, grate 1 teaspoon fresh ginger and squeeze the juice into the sauce.

- Add 1 or 2 drops of hot sauce or a pinch of cayenne pepper for a spicy zing.

Tahini-Lemon Sauce

This rich lemony sauce goes especially well with Middle Eastern-style dishes, like the Falafel Pockets (page 147), Mediterranean Rice and Barley Salad (page 43), and the Asparagus-Chickpea-Brown Rice Stir-Fry (page 151). It also makes a delicious topping for brown rice udon noodles and most grain and bean burgers.

Yield: About 1¼ cups

6 tablespoons tahini

½ cup water

2 tablespoons fresh lemon juice

2 tablespoon finely grated red or yellow onion

1 tablespoon chopped fresh parsley

1 clove garlic, minced

¼ teaspoon sea salt

1. Place all of the ingredients in a blender and pulse several seconds until well blended.

2. Use immediately, or store in an airtight container and refrigerate up to one week.

Citrus Vinaigrette

This fresh-tasting garlicky vinaigrette pairs well with many rice dishes, and adds great flavor to green salads, as well as cooked vegetables. It is featured in the Fiesta Salad on page 47.

1. Place all of the ingredients in a medium bowl and whisk until well blended.

2. Use immediately or store in an airtight container and refrigerate up to one week.

Yield: About 1 cup

$1/4$ cup extra virgin olive oil

$1/4$ cup brown rice or apple cider vinegar

$1/4$ cup fresh lime or lemon juice

$1/4$ cup water

I clove garlic, minced

I tablespoon minced fresh basil or mint, or I teaspoon dried

$1/4$ teaspoon sea salt

$1/4$ teaspoon black pepper

Mustard-Lemon Dressing

The perfectly paired flavors of mustard and lemon make this sauce a great match for fried foods like Brown Rice and Corn Fritters (page 78) and Rice and Buckwheat Croquettes (page 79). And be sure to try it as a dip for Golden Rice & Millet Nuggets (page 84).

1. Place all of the ingredients in a medium bowl and whisk until well blended.

2. Use immediately or store in an airtight container and refrigerate up to one week.

Yield: About 1 cup

$1/2$ cup balsamic vinegar

$1/2$ cup extra virgin olive oil

$2^1/2$ teaspoons Dijon-style mustard

2 teaspoon finely chopped fresh basil

$1/2$ teaspoon sea salt

$1/4$ teaspoon black pepper

FOR A CHANGE . . .

● For a different flavor, use chopped fresh mint in place of the basil.

Mushroom-Onion Sauce

Rich with earthy mushrooms and sweet onions, this flavorful gravy adds savory goodness to a wide variety of brown rice dishes—from pilafs and grain salads to burgers and simple sides. Because it is thickened with kuzu rather than flour, this sauce is an excellent choice for those who are gluten intolerant.

Yield: About 4 cups

2 tablespoons extra virgin olive oil

1¼ cups chopped onions

1 clove garlic, minced

1 cup sliced button mushrooms

½ cup sliced fresh shiitake mushroom caps

2 tablespoons kuzu root starch

2 tablespoons cold water

2 cups Vegetable Stock (page 48) or commercial variety

2½ teaspoons shoyu soy sauce, or ½ teaspoon sea salt

2 tablespoons minced chives, parsley, or scallions

1. Heat the oil in a medium skillet over medium heat. Add the onions and garlic, and sauté for 2 to 3 minutes or until beginning to soften. Add the mushrooms, and continue to sauté another 4 to 5 minutes or until they begin to release their moisture.

2. Dissolve the kuzu in the cold water and set aside.

3. Add the stock to the skillet, increase the heat, and bring to a boil. Reduce the heat to medium, then add the kuzu while stirring constantly. Cook for 2 to 3 minutes or until the sauce thickens.

4. Reduce the heat to low, add the shoyu, and cover. Stirring often, simmer for 7 to 10 minutes.

5. Remove from the heat, stir in the chives, and use immediately. Refrigerate leftover gravy in an airtight container up to three days.

FOR A CHANGE . . .

• For a richer, slightly nutty flavor, add 1 teaspoon toasted sesame oil in Step 1.

Mushroom Gravy

*Rich and savory, this fresh mushroom gravy
is a welcome topper for just about any rice dish.*

1. Heat the oil in a medium skillet over medium heat. Add the onions and garlic, and sauté for 2 to 3 minutes or until beginning to soften. Add the mushrooms and salt, and continue to sauté another 4 to 5 minutes or until the mushrooms begin to release their moisture.

2. Reduce the heat to medium-low. Sprinkle the flour into the skillet, and stir constantly until the onions and mushrooms are completely coated.

3. Combine the stock and soymilk, then add it *very slowly* to the skillet, while whisking or stirring constantly. Cook for 3 to 5 minutes or until the sauce thickens.

4. Reduce the heat to low, add the pepper, and cover. Stirring often, simmer for 7 to 10 minutes.

5. Remove from the heat, stir in the parsley, and use immediately. Refrigerate leftover gravy in an airtight container up to three days.

FOR A CHANGE . . .

- For added richness, substitute 1 tablespoon shoyu soy sauce for the salt.

Yield: 3½ to 4 cups

3 tablespoons extra virgin olive oil

½ cup finely diced onions
or shallots

1 clove garlic, minced

1 cup diced fresh button
mushrooms

1 cup diced fresh crimini
mushrooms

½ teaspoon sea salt, or to taste

¼ cup unbleached white or
whole wheat pastry flour

2 cups Vegetable Stock (page 48)
or commercial variety

1 cup plain unsweetened soymilk

¼ teaspoon black pepper

2 tablespoons minced fresh parsley,
chives, or scallions

A Little Rice Trivia . . .

With the exception of Antarctica, rice
is grown on every continent, and over
1 billion people are involved in its cultivation.

Soy Buttermilk

Yield: About 1¼ cups (equivalent to 1 medium egg)

1 cup unsweetened soymilk

1½ tablespoons apple cider vinegar or brown rice vinegar

2 tablespoons safflower, sunflower, or extra virgin olive oil

This soy buttermilk, which is called for in a number of recipes in this book, is an outstanding alternative to eggs in most baked goods. Although it calls for vinegar, the taste of vinegar is virtually undetectable in the finished product. For more information, see "Using Soy Buttermilk" below.

1. Combine all of the ingredients in a small bowl or measuring cup and stir well.

2. Let the mixture sit for 7 to 10 minutes or until it begins to form curds.

3. The soy buttermilk is now ready to use.

USING SOY BUTTERMILK

I prefer not to use eggs and I don't like recommending them. I have found soy buttermilk, to be an excellent egg replacer when making pancakes and waffles (see the recipes in Chapter 2), as well as muffins, cakes, and many other baked goods. It is a cholesterol-free, healthy alternative to most commercial egg replacers, which contain preservatives, stabilizers, food colorings, and other chemicals.

A word of advice—don't make soy buttermilk in large batches. Unlike dairy buttermilk, it sours easily (due to the vinegar) and does not keep well. It is best to prepare it in small quantities as called for in a recipe and use right away.

Quick Homemade Rice Milk

Homemade rice milk is very different tasting than commercial varieties. It is also very easy to make. Enjoy it as a beverage or use it on Muesli (page 37), Granola (page 35), or your favorite cereal.

1. Place the brown rice flakes in a blender and grind to a fine powder. Add the remaining ingredients and pulse several seconds until thoroughly blended.

2. Transfer the pulpy mixture to a large bowl and let sit for 5 to 7 minutes.

3. Place a fine mesh sieve or strainer over a clean empty bowl. Line the sieve with a double layer of unbleached cotton cheesecloth.

4. Pour the rice mixture into the lined sieve. Gather the ends of the cheesecloth together to form a sack, then squeeze out the rice milk. (The pulp will be trapped within the sack.)

5. Transfer the milk to a glass bottle or jar, seal, and refrigerate. It will keep about one week.

Yield: About 6 cups

1 cup brown rice cereal flakes

6 cups cold water

1 pinch sea salt

2 tablespoons brown rice syrup

FOR A CHANGE . . .

- For flavored milk, include 1 teaspoon vanilla extract to the ingredients.
- To give the milk a slight maple taste, substitute 1 tablespoon maple syrup for the brown rice syrup.
- For a different tasting, richer flavor, use $1/2$ cup brown rice flakes and $1/2$ cup rolled oats.

Tofu Sour Cream

Yield: About 2 cups

1 pound extra-firm tofu, rinsed and drained

1/3 cup water

1 tablespoon fresh lemon juice

1 tablespoon brown rice vinegar or apple cider vinegar

1 clove garlic, minced

2 teaspoons umeboshi vinegar, or 1/4 teaspoon sea salt

1/3 cup chopped fresh chives or parsley

Cool and creamy, this rich sour cream goes especially well with spicy Mexican-style dishes like burritos and enchiladas. Add a dollop to Mexican Black Beans and Rice (page 122), Lentil Rice Soup (page 53), and the Middle-Eastern classic Mujaddarah (page 134).

1. Place all of the ingredients in a blender, and pulse until smooth and creamy. If too thick, add more water *a little at a time* to reach the desired consistency.

2. Use immediately or refrigerate and serve chilled.

3. Store leftover sour cream in an airtight container and refrigerate up to five days.

Blueberry-Peach Syrup

Yield: About 2 1/2 cups

2 cups fresh blueberries

1 1/2 tablespoons maple syrup, or to taste

1/2 cup thinly sliced fresh peaches or nectarines

1/4 cup chopped roasted walnuts (optional)

Want to elevate your pancakes, waffles, and hot cereal to delicious new heights? Top them with this colorful, fruity sauce.

1. Place the blueberries and the maple syrup in a blender, and purée until smooth. Transfer to a small serving bowl.

2. Add the sliced peaches and walnuts (if using) to the bowl, and mix well before serving.

Lemon-Walnut Syrup

*Roasted walnuts add flavor and crunch to this lemony syrup.
Drizzle it warm or at room temperature over pancakes
and waffles.*

1. Place the brown rice syrup, water, lemon juice, and lemon zest in a small saucepan over medium-low heat. Stir well and heat until just beginning to boil.

2. Remove from the heat, add the walnuts, and transfer to a small serving bowl. Mix well and serve.

FOR A CHANGE . . .

- Use roasted pecans or other nuts in place of the walnuts.
- Instead of brown rice syrup, use maple syrup or honey.
- Try different citrus juices in place of or in combination with the lemon juice.

Yield: About 1$\frac{1}{3}$ cups

$\frac{1}{2}$ cup brown rice syrup

$\frac{1}{4}$ cup cold water

$\frac{1}{4}$ cup fresh lemon juice, or to taste

$\frac{1}{2}$ teaspoon lemon zest

$\frac{1}{3}$ cup coarsely chopped roasted walnuts

Strawberry-Blueberry Sauce

*Enjoy this luscious fruity sauce on pancakes and waffles,
crisp rice cakes, and your favorite puddings.*

1. Place 1$\frac{1}{2}$ cups of the strawberries and the maple syrup in a blender, and purée until smooth. Transfer to a small serving bowl.

2. Slice the remaining $\frac{1}{2}$ cup strawberries, and add them to the bowl along with the blueberries. Mix well and serve.

Yield: About 2$\frac{1}{2}$ cups

2 cups fresh strawberries

$\frac{1}{3}$ cup fresh blueberries

1$\frac{1}{2}$ tablespoons maple syrup, or to taste

5

Appetizers

Whether served as a prelude to a meal, a treat to share with guests, or an any-time snack, appetizers are always welcomed. In this chapter, I'll be sharing some of my all-time brown-rice favorites with you.

Brown rice has always been among my family's staple foods—one that we've enjoyed on a regular basis. Whenever leftovers were available, I tried my best to turn those cooked grains into new dishes for my family's continued enjoyment. And over the years, I discovered hundreds of ways to use that leftover rice, either alone or in combination with beans and/or other grains. Many of the taste-tempting appetizers on the following pages are among those creations.

My children (and grandchildren) have always been great fans of the bite-sized Brown Rice and Corn Fritters, Rice and Buckwheat Croquettes, and Quick 'n Easy Samosas. For this reason, I've often served them as side dishes with dinner. This chapter also includes many other delicious appetizers, including savory Stuffed Mushrooms and traditional Japanese Rice Balls, to name just a few. Be sure to try the deep-fried Crispy Rice Noodles (made with brown rice udon)—they make a wonderful snack with lots of crunch.

With the growing popularity of sushi—and sushi rolls in particular—I have dedicated an entire section to these Japanese favorites. I will show you how to make perfect sushi rice, suggest the best fillings, and then present easy-to-follow instructions for forming the rolls. To ensure successful results, clear instructional drawings will guide you every step of the way.

So if you're looking for something special to serve guests, or you simply want to offer your family a healthy appetizing snack, you'll find plenty of choices in this chapter.

Brown Rice and Corn Fritters

*Rich, sweet, and deeply satisfying, corn fritters are a Southern
classic. Although most require eggs, this vegan variation calls
for either cholesterol-free kuzu root starch or arrowroot
to perform the same binding function. Both products
also thicken like cornstarch, but unlike cornstarch,
they are GMO free and contain no chemicals.*

Yield: 18 to 20 fritters

1 1/2 cups fresh or frozen sweet corn

1 1/2 cups cooked short-,
medium-, or long-grain brown rice
(page 19)

1/2 cup whole wheat pastry or
unbleached white flour

1 tablespoon cornmeal

1 1/2 teaspoons baking powder

1/4 cup minced red bell pepper

1 teaspoon kuzu root starch
or arrowroot

1/4 teaspoon ground cumin

1/4 teaspoon sea salt

1/4 teaspoon black pepper

3/4 cup water or
plain unsweetened soymilk

Safflower oil for frying

1. Place all of the ingredients except the water and oil in
a medium mixing bowl and stir until well combined. While
continuing to stir, slowly add enough water to form a
slightly firm (not watery) batter.

2. Heat 3 to 4 tablespoons of oil in a large heavy skillet
over medium-high heat. Drop about 1 heaping tablespoon
of batter onto the hot skillet and flatten lightly with the
back of a spoon to the thickness of a pancake. Continue
adding batter to the skillet, leaving about an inch of space
between them.

3. Cook the fritters about 3 to 4 minutes on each side or
until golden brown. Remove and place on paper towels to
absorb any oil.

4. Transfer the fritters to a platter and enjoy plain or
with a drizzle of Roasted Red Pepper Sauce (page 65),
Mustard-Lemon Dressing (page 69), or Pineapple Salsa
(page 63).

FOR A CHANGE . . .

- Instead of using brown rice only, try a combination of brown rice and wild
  rice, or brown rice and cooked beans.
- For a spicy kick, add 1/8 teaspoon cayenne pepper in place of (or in combination with) the cumin.

Rice and Buckwheat Croquettes

These delicious bite-sized croquettes are a favorite in my home, especially when served with a pungent dipping sauce. I sometimes form the mixture into larger croquettes and serve them with dinner as a side dish or even as a main course. Make sure the grains are cool or at room temperature—hot grains don't hold together well.

1. Place the rice, buckwheat, onion, carrots, parsley, and 2 tablespoons flour in a medium mixing bowl, and stir to thoroughly combine. Form the mixture into $1\frac{1}{2}$-inch balls. Roll the balls in a little flour to evenly coat and set aside.

2. Heat about 2 inches of oil in a deep fryer or medium pot over medium-high heat.

3. Once the oil is hot, reduce the heat slightly, and carefully drop a few croquettes into the pot. Do not add too many at once—this will cause the temperature of the oil to drop and result in oil-soaked croquettes that don't hold together well.

4. Fry the croquettes about 3 to 5 minutes or until golden brown. As they cook, turn them once or twice with tongs or a spoon. Remove and place on paper towels to absorb any oil.

5. Set a bowl with the shoyu-ginger sauce in the middle of a serving platter. Surround with croquettes and serve.

Yield: About 16 croquettes

I cup cooked short-grain brown rice, cool or at room temperature (page 19)

I cup cooked buckwheat, cool or at room temperature

$\frac{1}{4}$ cup minced red onion

$\frac{1}{4}$ cup minced carrots

$\frac{1}{4}$ cup minced fresh parsley or chives

2 tablespoons whole wheat pastry flour

Whole wheat pastry flour for coating croquettes

Safflower oil for frying

Shoyu-Ginger Sauce (page 62)

FOR A CHANGE . . .

- Substitute any leftover brown rice cooked with other grains, such as millet, quinoa, wild rice, barley, etc.; or even leftover brown rice and bean combinations.

- Try the croquettes with Pineapple Salsa (page 63), Mustard-Lemon Dressing (page 69), or Sweet and Sour Sauce (page 64).

Quick 'n Easy Samosas

Samosas are deep-fried or baked pastries that generally contain a savory filling. Although they are traditional Indian fare, samosas are popular in many parts of the world, where they are known by different names. This easy-to-make version uses prepared wonton wrappers instead of heavy pastry dough.

Yield: About 32 samosas

1 1/2 cups cooked short-, medium-, or long-grain brown rice (page 19)

1/2 cup cooked lentils

1/3 cup raisins, currants, or dried cranberries

1/2 teaspoon curry powder

1/4 teaspoon ground cumin

16-ounce package wonton wrappers (about 32)

Safflower oil for frying

Honey-Mustard Sauce (page 65)

1. Place the rice, lentils, raisins, curry powder, and cumin in a medium bowl and mix until well combined.

2. Fill a small bowl with cold water and set aside. Lay a wonton wrapper on a clean flat surface and place 1 heaping teaspoon of rice mixture in the center. Dip your fingers in the water and moisten the edges of the wrapper. Take one corner and fold it over the filling to the opposite corner to form a triangle. Firmly press the edges together to seal. Repeat with the remaining wrappers.

3. Heat about 2 inches of oil in a deep fryer or medium pot over medium-high heat. Adding a few samosas at a time (do not crowd the pot), deep-fry for 3 to 4 minutes or until golden brown. Remove and place on paper towels to absorb any oil.

4. Arrange the samosas on a platter and serve with the honey-mustard dipping sauce.

FOR A CHANGE . . .

• Substitute phyllo or puff pastry dough for the wonton wrappers. If using phyllo, bake the samosas in a 375°F oven for 15 to 20 minutes or until golden brown. For puff pastry, bake in a 400°F oven for 10 minutes, then reduce the heat to 375°F and bake another 10 minutes or until browned.

• Try these samosas with Shoyu-Ginger Sauce (page 62), Pineapple Salsa (page 63), Sweet and Sour Sauce (page 64), or your favorite chutney.

Stuffed Mushrooms

*Filled with a flavorful seasoned rice stuffing,
these savory mushroom caps are always a hit!*

1. Preheat the oven to 350°F. Remove the stems from the mushrooms and set the caps aside. Save the stems for another use.

2. Heat the oil in a small skillet over medium-low heat. Add the shallots and garlic, and sauté for 3 to 5 minutes or until beginning to soften. Transfer to a medium bowl.

3. Add all of the remaining ingredients except the soy sauce to the bowl. Mix well.

4. Stuff each mushroom cap with about 1 tablespoon of the rice mixture. Sprinkle with 1 or 2 drops of shoyu, and arrange on a baking sheet.

5. Bake for 15 to 20 minutes or until the mochi is melted and the mushrooms are tender. If desired, place under the broiler during the last minute or so to brown the stuffing slightly.

6. Transfer the caps to a serving platter and enjoy warm or at room temperature.

FOR A CHANGE . . .

- Instead of all brown rice, use a combination of brown and wild rice.
- Add ¼ cup minced seitan to the filling mixture.

Yield: 8 to 10 stuffed mushrooms

8 to 10 large white button "stuffing" mushrooms

1 to 2 tablespoons extra virgin olive oil

¼ cup minced shallots or onion

1 clove garlic, minced

1 cup cooked short-, medium-, or long-grain brown rice (page 19)

1 cup coarse whole wheat breadcrumbs

¼ cup coarsely grated mochi

¼ cup plain unsweetened soymilk or water

2 tablespoons minced sauerkraut

1 tablespoon minced fresh parsley

½ teaspoon lemon zest

¼ teaspoon ground sage or poultry seasoning

Shoyu soy sauce to taste

Dolmades
Stuffed Grape Leaves

Popular in Greece and throughout the Middle East, these stuffed grape leaves are typically filled with white rice, finely chopped vegetables, and/or ground meat. This nutritious vegetarian version is made with brown rice and lentils. Preparing dolmades is a bit tedious, but well worth the effort. You can also make them several days in advance. Dolmades are usually served with a yogurt dipping sauce.

1. Rinse the grape leaves under cold water. Place in a bowl, cover with warm water, and let soak about 1 hour.

2. Fill a medium-size pot about halfway with water and bring to a boil. Add the grape leaves and blanch for 1 minute. Drain the leaves and pat dry with paper towels. Remove and discard the stems, then set the leaves aside.

3. Place the vegetable stock, lemon juice, olive oil, mint, and zest in a bowl. Stir well and set aside.

4. To prepare the filling, combine the rice and lentils in a medium mixing bowl, and set aside. Heat the oil in a medium skillet over medium-low heat. Add the onions and garlic, and sauté for 2 to 3 minutes or until they begin to soften. Add to the rice-lentil mixture along with the remaining filling ingredients. Stir until well combined.

5. To prepare the dolmades, place 1 grape leaf on a flat surface, vein side up. (If the leaves are small, place 2 leaves so they overlap.) Place about $1^1/_2$ tablespoons of filling in the center of the leaf near the base (see Step 1 at right). Fold the bottom of the leaf over the filling (see Step 2), then fold the right and left sides of the leaf toward the center (see Step 3).

Yield: About 24 dolmades

15.2-ounce jar grape leaves (packed in vinegar brine)

2 cups Vegetable Stock (page 48) or commercial variety

$^1/_4$ cup fresh lemon juice

3 tablespoons extra virgin olive oil

2 teaspoons minced fresh mint

2 teaspoons lemon zest

FILLING

2 cups cooked long-grain brown rice (page 19)

1 cup cooked lentils, well drained

1 tablespoon extra virgin olive oil

$^1/_3$ cup minced onion or shallots

1 clove garlic, minced

1 teaspoon ground cumin

$^1/_4$ teaspoon ground cinnamon or allspice

$^1/_4$ teaspoon sea salt

$^1/_8$ teaspoon black pepper

6. Roll up the leaf to form a neat "package" (see Step 4). It should be shaped like a small egg roll. Continue with the remaining leaves and filling.

7. Arrange a single layer of the dolmades in the bottom of a medium pot. Top with another layer, placing them in the opposite direction of the layer below. Continue layering.

8. Pour the vegetable stock mixture over the dolmades. Place a heat-proof plate inside the pot so that it rests on top of the stuffed leaves. Cover the pot with a sheet of foil, add the lid, then bring to a boil over high heat. Reduce the heat to medium-low and cook for about 1 hour. Turn off the heat and let rest for 10 to 15 minutes. Do not uncover.

9. Remove the dolmades, drain well, and let cool. Serve at room temperature or refrigerate and enjoy chilled. Store leftovers in a sealed container in the refrigerator up to two weeks.

FOR A CHANGE . . .

- Substitute a combination of rice and other grains for the brown rice.
- Use cooked chickpeas instead of lentils.
- Add $\frac{1}{4}$ cup finely chopped fresh tomato to the filling mixture.

1. Place the filling near the base of the leaf (where the stem had been).

2. Fold the bottom of the leaf over the filling.

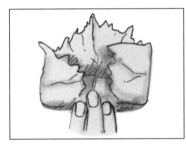

3. Fold the right and left sides of the leaf toward the center.

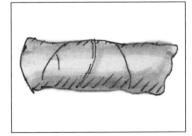

4. Roll up the leaf to form a neat package (like a small egg roll).

Golden Rice & Millet Nuggets

The deep golden color and delicate sweet flavor of these tasty nuggets come from the squash, which also acts as a binder. When preparing this dish, keep in mind that hot grains don't hold together well, so be sure the mixture has cooled to room temperature before forming the nuggets. Using cold leftover rice is even better.

Yield: 24 to 32 nuggets

I cup short-grain brown rice, rinsed and drained

I cup millet, rinsed and drained

1 1/2 cups cubed buttercup squash or Hokkaido pumpkin (peeled)

4 1/2 cups water

I pinch sea salt

I cup panko breadcrumbs or fine cornmeal

Safflower oil for frying

1. Place all of the ingredients except the panko and oil in a medium pot. Cover and bring to a boil over high heat.

2. Reduce the heat to medium-low, stir once, and cover. Simmer for 45 to 50 minutes, or until the liquid is absorbed and the grains are tender. Remove from the heat, let sit for 10 minutes, then transfer to a mixing bowl. Fluff with a fork and let cool to room temperature.

3. Mash the cooled mixture together with your hands or a potato masher until well combined.

4. Moisten your hands slightly in warm water, and form the mixture into 1 1/2-inch balls. Roll the balls in panko to evenly coat.

5. Heat 2 to 3 inches of oil in a deep fryer or medium pot over medium-high heat. Add 4 to 5 nuggets at a time (do not crowd the pot), and deep-fry for 3 to 4 minutes or until golden brown. Remove and place on paper towels to absorb any oil.

6. Arrange the nuggets on a platter and serve plain or with your favorite dipping sauce. The Peanut-Mustard Sauce (page 68), Shoyu-Ginger Sauce (page 62), and Honey-Mustard Sauce (page 65) are all recommended choices.

- For added protein, include some cooked pinto, azuki, kidney, or black beans to the rice-millet mixture.

- Enjoy these nuggets as a side dish topped with Mushroom Gravy (page 71) or Sweet and Sour Sauce (page 64).

Crispy Rice Noodles

Although these crunchy brown rice noodles are recommended with Vegetable Chow Mein (page 157), you can also serve them as a simple snack plain or with a dip. My family usually enjoys them with Peanut-Mustard Sauce (page 68), Sweet and Sour Sauce (page 64), or Wasabi-Shoyu Dipping Sauce (page 62).

1. Cook the noodles according to package directions. Rinse and let drain at least 2 hours.

2. Heat about 3 inches of oil in a deep fryer or medium pot over medium-high heat.

3. When the oil is hot, add about one-fourth of the noodles and deep-fry for 3 to 5 minutes or until golden brown. Remove and place on paper towels to absorb any oil. Continue to deep-fry the remaining noodles.

4. Serve plain or with your favorite dipping sauce.

FOR A CHANGE . . .

- For even thinner crispy noodles, use brown rice bifun noodles or vermicelli.

Yield: 3 to 4 servings

8 ounces brown rice udon noodles or spaghetti

Safflower oil for frying

Japanese Rice Balls

When making rice balls, it is best to use leftover rice—cool or at room temperature—which holds together better than rice that is freshly made. Although this basic recipe calls for the rice to be shaped into balls, feel free to form other shapes (see the inset on page 87). Also, the balls are covered with toasted nori, but be sure to check the "For a change" entries at right for other delicious coating ideas.

Yield: 2 rice balls

1 sheet toasted nori

1 medium umeboshi plum, cut in half

2 cups cooked short-grain brown rice, cool or at room temperature* (page 19)

* You can also use a combination of short- and medium-grain rice.

1. Cut or fold the nori into four equal pieces. Set aside.

2. Wet your hands very slightly with cold water. Scoop up half the rice and firmly pack it into a ball.

3. Press a hole into the center of the ball with your finger. Place a piece of umeboshi inside, then pack the ball again to close the hole (see Step 1 below).

4. Place a square of nori on one side of the rice ball. With a slightly wet hand, press the nori against the ball so it sticks. Repeat with another square of nori on the other side to completely cover the ball (see Step 2). Form a second rice ball with the remaining ingredients.

1. Place a piece of umeboshi inside the ball.

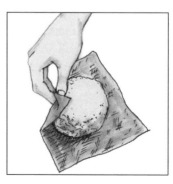

2. Cover the ball with nori.

Preparing Rice Balls

5. Serve the rice balls whole (to be eaten like apples) or cut them in half or quarters.

6. To serve at a later time, place the balls in a paper towel-lined covered container, and refrigerate up to three days.

FOR A CHANGE . . .

- Substitute pieces of pickled ginger or small chunks of pickled daikon radish for the umeboshi.

- You can make four smaller golf ball-sized rice balls instead of two larger ones. Cover each with two smaller strips of nori.

- Instead of nori, roll the balls in Gomashio (page 67) or toasted sesame seeds.

ABOUT JAPANESE RICE BALLS

Japanese rice balls—called *onigiri* or *musubi*—are great for using up leftover rice. Sticky short-grain varieties are best, although a combination of short- and medium-grain rice works, too.

The rice is commonly formed into triangular mounds, round balls, or small cylinders (called bales). A piece of pickled ginger, umeboshi plum, or pickled daikon radish is often stuffed into the center before they are completely or partially wrapped in nori.

Although rice balls last longer when kept cool, they also keep well outside the refrigerator. This makes them great snack choices for lunch boxes and to take along when traveling.

Be sure to try the basic recipe at left, as well the Azuki Rice Balls on page 88 and the Firecracker Mini Rice Balls on page 89.

Round ball

Cylinder-shaped bale

Triangular mound

Azuki Rice Balls

These rich-tasting appetizers, made with azuki beans and brown rice, are always a hit in my home. I form them into cylinder-shaped "bales" and then pan-fry. Delicious!

Yield: 4 bales

2 cups cooked Azuki Bean Rice (page 113), cool or at room temperature*

1 to 2 tablespoons plain or toasted sesame oil

1/2 teaspoon shoyu soy sauce (optional)

* Can also use 1 1/2 cups cooked short-grain brown rice and 1/2 cup cooked azuki beans.

1. Place the azuki bean rice in a medium bowl. Scoop up one-fourth of the mixture and form it into a firmly packed cylinder-shaped bale (about 1 inch thick and 2 inches long). Form 3 more bales with the remaining rice mixture.

2. Heat the oil in a medium skillet over medium-high heat. Add the bales and fry about 5 to 7 minutes or until golden brown on the bottom. Sprinkle with 1 or 2 drops of shoyu (if using), then turn the bales over and continue to fry until browned. Remove and place on paper towels to absorb any oil.

3. Transfer to a serving platter and enjoy hot, warm, or at room temperature.

FOR A CHANGE . . .

● Add 1/4 to 1/3 cup minced chives, scallions, or onions to the rice-azuki bean mixture.

● Roll the bales in toasted sesame seeds before frying.

Rice is nice . . . for a good night's sleep.

If you have trouble falling asleep or staying asleep through the night, try filling a neck pillow with raw brown rice . . . and enjoy a deep peaceful slumber.

Firecracker Mini Rice Balls

If you're in the mood for a five-alarm appetizer or snack, look no further. These fiery bites get their intense burst of heat from a spicy jalapeño mixture, and their nutty crunch from a rich coating of toasted sesame seeds. One word of advice—when serving these little "firecrackers," be sure to have an icy cold beverage nearby.

1. Place the rice in a medium mixing bowl. Place the sesame seeds in a small bowl. Set aside.

2. Add all of the dipping sauce ingredients to a small bowl and mix well. Set aside.

3. Heat the olive oil in a small skillet over medium heat. Add the bell peppers, jalapeños, and garlic, and sauté for 3 to 5 minutes or until soft. Add to the rice and mix well.

4. Lightly moisten your hands with cold water. Scoop up 2 tablespoons of the rice mixture, form it into a golf ball-size round, and place on a platter or baking sheet. Continue forming balls with the remaining rice.

5. Roll the balls in sesame seeds to coat. Set aside.

6. Heat about 3-inches of oil in a medium pot or deep fryer over medium-high heat. Add 3 to 5 balls at a time (don't crowd the pot), and deep-fry for 3 to 4 minutes, or until golden. Remove and place on paper towels to absorb any oil.

7. Place the bowl of dipping sauce in the middle of a platter, surround with rice balls, and serve!

Yield: About 24 mini rice balls

3 cups cooked short-grain brown rice (page 19), cool or at room temperature

$^3/_4$ cup toasted sesame seeds

2 teaspoons olive oil

$^1/_4$ cup minced red bell peppers

3 tablespoons minced jalapeño peppers

2 cloves garlic, minced

Safflower oil for frying

SPICY DIPPING SAUCE

$^1/_2$ cup cold water

3 tablespoons shoyu soy sauce

1 tablespoon Tabasco or other hot sauce

FOR A CHANGE . . .

● Omit the jalapeño mixture, form the balls, and poke a hole in the center of each with your index finger. Fill each ball with $^1/_4$ teaspoon wasabi paste and $^1/_4$ teaspoon umeboshi paste. Pack the balls firmly with slightly moistened hands to close up the holes before rolling in sesame seeds.

Sushi Rice

Most sushi today is made with white sushi rice that is seasoned with vinegar and white sugar. This healthier version is made with short-grain brown rice, and flavored with traditional seasonings—brown rice vinegar and mirin (sweet rice cooking wine). This recipe yields enough rice to make 4 to 5 sushi rolls.

Yield: 5½ to 6 cups

2 cups short-grain brown rice, rinse and drained

4 cups cold water

1 pinch sea salt

3 tablespoons brown rice vinegar

3 tablespoons mirin, or a combination of brown rice and maple syrup

1. Place the rice, water, and salt in a heavy medium pot. Cover and bring to a boil over high heat. Reduce the heat to medium-low, stir once, and cover. Simmer for 45 to 50 minutes or until the liquid is absorbed and the rice is tender. Remove from the heat, and let sit for 10 minutes.

2. Transfer the rice to a large bowl (wooden is recommended). To smooth out the rice, cut through it very gently with a bamboo rice paddle or wooden spatula. Do not stir or mix the rice, which will make it mushy and cause it to clump.

3. Heat the vinegar and mirin in a small pot, but do not boil. Pour the hot mixture over the rice. To combine the rice and vinegar, once again, gently cut through the mixture until the rice is well coated. Let cool to room temperature. You can also cover the rice loosely with wax paper and let sit unrefrigerated overnight.

4. The sushi rice is now ready to use according to the recipe.*

* It is best to use sushi rice shortly after it's made. I do not recommend refrigeration, which changes its taste and texture. If refrigeration is necessary, be sure the rice is in a sealed container and let it come to room temp before using. Also, use it within a day, as the vinegar will cause the rice to sour quickly.

FOR A CHANGE . . .

● Omit adding the brown rice vinegar and mirin. Sushi rice that is made without vinegar and sweetener will last a day or two longer.

WHAT YOU SHOULD KNOW ABOUT SUSHI

When some people hear the word sushi, they automatically think of raw fish. But sushi actually refers to a number of different dishes that are made with sushi rice—a short-grain sticky rice that is flavored with sweetened vinegar (see the recipe on page 90). Some sushi varieties contain fish, but not all.

In the United States, sushi rolls, called *nori-maki* or *maki zushi,* are steadily growing in popularity. They contain sushi rice and other ingredients (typically vegetables and/or fish) that are rolled up in a sheet of toasted nori. The roll is then cut into small rounds, which are usually served with a dab of pungent wasabi paste, a sprinkle of soy sauce, and/or some slices of pickled ginger. The basic Nori-Maki recipe beginning on page 92 offers clear step-by-step instructions along with helpful illustrations to help guide you in making these Japanese favorites.

In addition to rolls, *nigiri zushi* is another popular type of sushi in which the rice is formed into small compressed cylinders called *bales,* and then topped with cooked shrimp or thin slices of raw fish. For *temaki zushi,* the rice and other ingredients are wrapped in a sheet of nori that is rolled into a cone shape. It is picked up and eaten by hand like an ice cream cone. For *chirashi zushi,* often called "scattered sushi," the rice is served in a bowl and topped with a colorful array of ingredients—usually vegetables (see the recipe on page 46).

Sushi is quick and easy to make. Be sure to use white sushi rice, Arborio, or short-grain brown rice that has cooled to room temperature. Don't use freshly made hot rice—the roll will fall apart. To form the rolls, you will need a sushi mat, although a woven placemat can work, too. Be aware that unlike rice balls, sushi must be kept cold to prevent spoilage.

Finally, if you are using fish in your sushi, I strongly advise using cooked seafood only, such as shrimp, crab, and smoked fish. If raw fish is not sushi quality—and much of it is not—it can make you sick. Leave raw fish to the expert sushi chefs, who are well trained in knowing how to choose sushi-quality seafood.

Nori-maki

Temaki zushi

Nigiri zushi

Popular sushi varieties

Nori-Maki
Sushi Rolls

Nori-maki is the Japanese name for nori-wrapped sushi rolls of which there are many varieties. This basic recipe includes helpful illustrations to guide you in their preparation.

1. Slice the carrot lengthwise into ¼-inch-thick strips and blanch in boiling water for 2 to 3 minutes. Remove, rinse under cold water, and set aside.

2. Remove the ends from the cucumbers and slice lengthwise into ¼ to ½-inch-thick strips and set aside.

3. Place a sheet of nori (smooth, shiny side down) on a sushi mat. Spread one-fourth of the rice over the nori, leaving a 1-inch border at the bottom and 2-inch border at the top. Flatten the rice firmly with a slightly wet bamboo rice paddle or wooden spatula.

4. Place a row of sliced carrots and cucumbers lengthwise across the center of the rice (see Step 1 below).

Yield: 4 sushi rolls
(32 pieces)

1 small carrot

1 small cucumber

4 sheets toasted nori

1 recipe Sushi Rice (page 90), at room temperature

GARNISH OPTIONS

Wasabi paste

Pickled ginger slices

Shoyu soy sauce

Wasabi-Shoyu Dipping Sauce (page 62)

Preparing Sushi Rolls

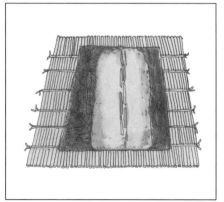

1. Spread the rice on the sheet of nori. Top with carrot and cucumber strips.

5. Lightly moisten the top border of the nori with water, then, starting at the bottom, roll up the nori using the sushi mat (see Step 2). Press gently but firmly while rolling.

6. Continue making rolls with the remaining nori and filling. If you are not serving the sushi right away, place the uncut rolls on a platter, cover with plastic wrap, and refrigerate. This will prevent the rolls from drying out.

7. Just before serving, place a roll on a cutting surface, lightly moisten a sharp knife, and slice the roll in half. Moisten the knife slightly again, and cut each half in half. Once again, moisten the knife, and slice each quarter in half (see Step 3). This will yield 8 pieces.

8. Arrange the rounds on a platter and serve plain or with the recommended garnishes.

FOR A CHANGE . . .

- Instead of (or along with) cucumbers and carrots, add thin slices of avocado, scallions, or small cubes of pan-fried tofu to the filling. Just be careful not to cram the roll with too many ingredients. It won't roll up properly, and will result in pieces of sushi that are too large and difficult to eat with one or two bites.

2. Roll up the filled nori.

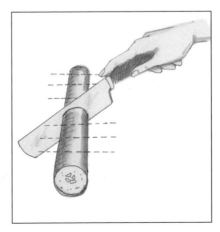

3. Slice the roll into rounds.

Tempeh Sushi Rolls

This is my absolute favorite sushi. Made with fried tempeh, sauerkraut, and lots of other flavorful ingredients, these rolls are a nourishing complete-protein snack, main dish, or appetizer.

Yield: 4 sushi rolls (32 pieces)

2 tablespoons extra virgin olive or safflower oil

1-pound block tempeh

1 cup water

1 1/2 tablespoons shoyu soy sauce

1 large carrot cut into long 1/4-inch-thick strips

1 recipe Sushi Rice (page 90), at room temperature

4 sheets toasted nori

4 scallions, roots removed

1/3 cup sauerkraut, drained well

1 tablespoon brown or yellow mustard

GARNISH OPTIONS

Wasabi paste

Pickled ginger slices

Shoyu soy sauce

Wasabi-Shoyu Dipping Sauce (page 62)

1. Heat the oil in a medium skillet over medium-high heat. Add the tempeh, and fry for 3 to 5 minutes on each side or until slightly browned. Add the water and shoyu, and bring to a boil. Cover, reduce the heat to medium-low, and simmer about 20 minutes. Uncover, increase the heat to high, and continue cooking about 5 minutes or until the liquid has cooked off.

2. While the tempeh is simmering, blanch the carrots and set aside. Slice the cooked tempeh lengthwise into long 1/4-inch-thick strips.

3. Place a sheet of nori (smooth, shiny side down) on a sushi mat. Spread about one-fourth of the rice on the nori, leaving a 1-inch border at the bottom and 2-inch border at the top. Flatten the rice firmly with a slightly wet bamboo rice paddle or wooden spatula.

4. Place 1 or 2 carrot strips lengthwise across the center of the rice. Next, add 1 or 2 tempeh strips, a scallion, and about 2 tablespoons of sauerkraut. Spread one-fourth of the mustard on the rice.

5. Lightly moisten the top border of the nori with water, then, starting at the bottom, roll up the nori using the sushi mat. Press gently but firmly while rolling.

6. Continue making rolls with the remaining nori and filling. If you are not serving the sushi right away, place the uncut rolls on a platter, cover with plastic wrap, and refrigerate. This will prevent the rolls from drying out.

7. Just before serving, place a roll on a cutting surface, lightly moisten a sharp knife, and slice the roll in half. Moisten the knife slightly again, and cut each half in half. Once again, moisten the knife, and slice each quarter in half. This will yield 8 pieces.

8. Arrange the rounds on a platter and serve plain or with the recommended garnishes.

FOR A CHANGE . . .

- Substitute strips of deep-fried tofu or cooked seitan for the tempeh.
- For a quicker version, use pan-fried strips of prepared tempeh bacon instead of tempeh that needs to be cooked.

Cucumber Sushi Rolls

*Also known as "kappa maki,"cucumber sushi
is one of the easiest to make.*

1. Place a sheet of nori (smooth, shiny side down) on a sushi mat. Spread about one-fourth of the rice on the nori, leaving a 1-inch border at the bottom and 2-inch border at the top. Flatten the rice firmly with a slightly wet bamboo rice paddle or wooden spatula.

2. Spread $1/4$ of the umeboshi paste in an even line lengthwise across the center of the rice. Top with 1 or 2 cucumber strips.

3. Lightly moisten the top border of the nori with water, then, starting at the bottom, roll up the nori using the sushi mat. Press gently but firmly while rolling.

4. Continue making rolls with the remaining nori and filling. If you are not serving the sushi right away, place the uncut rolls on a platter, cover with plastic wrap, and refrigerate. This will prevent the rolls from drying out.

5. Just before serving, place a roll on a cutting surface, lightly moisten a sharp knife, and slice the roll in half. Moisten the knife slightly again, and cut each half in half. Once again, moisten the knife, and slice each quarter in half. This will yield 8 pieces.

6. Arrange the rounds on a platter and serve plain or with the recommended garnishes.

Yield: 4 sushi rolls
(32 pieces)

4 sheets toasted nori

1 recipe Sushi Rice (page 90),
at room temperature

1 medium English cucumber,
unpeeled and cut lengthwise into
$1/2$-inch-thick slices

2 teaspoons umeboshi paste

GARNISH OPTIONS

Wasabi paste

Pickled ginger slices

Shoyu soy sauce

Wasabi-Shoyu Dipping Sauce
(page 62)

USING CHOPSTICKS

The first chopsticks—likely long twigs or sticks—were developed over 5,000 years ago in China. Initially used for stirring food in deep pots, chopsticks became eating utensils around 400 BC. At that time, due to China's growing population, natural resources had grown scarce. To conserve fuel, people began cutting food into small pieces, which cooked faster. Chopsticks, which pinched the tiny pieces of food between their tips, soon became the eating utensils of choice. By 500 AD, they were being used throughout Asia.

Using chopsticks is pretty easy once you get the hang of it. All it takes is a little practice. The following steps and helpful illustrations will help get you started. A word of advice—although chopsticks are usually held about midway, when first learning to use them, it is best to hold them closer to the bottom for better control.

Chopsticks are considered honorable utensils that should be treated respectfully. You should be aware of the rules of etiquette regarding their use. Although these rules vary from culture to culture, the following list includes a few actions that are considered rude and disrespectful by most. When eating with chopsticks, never:

❑ Stand them straight up in a bowl of rice.
❑ Use them to take food from a communal platter.
❑ Allow soup or other liquids to drip from them.
❑ Use them to spear food.
❑ Lick or chew on them.
❑ Use them to push away unwanted food or to pull a dish closer.
❑ Point with them.
❑ Rinse them off in your soup or beverage.
❑ Constantly hold them while dining.

When eating with chopsticks, keep in mind that they are more than just two sticks for picking up food. They are iconic symbols treasured by many cultures, and should be used with the utmost respect.

1. Place one chopstick between the base of your thumb and index finger. Rest the lower end against the tip of your ring finger. This stick should remain fixed.

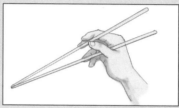

2. Place the other chopstick between the tips of your index and middle finger, and brace it with the tip of your thumb (as you would hold a pencil).

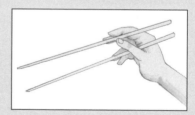

3. To separate the tips when picking up food, lift your index finger to raise the upper stick (keep the other one braced).

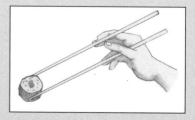

4. Move the stick downward to clamp the food between the tips of both sticks.

Shiitake and Avocado Sushi Rolls

Savory shoyu-simmered shiitake combine perfectly with the melt-in-your-mouth texture of rich, creamy avocado. Delicious!

1. Place the shiitake and water in a small pot, cover, and bring to a boil. Reduce the heat to medium-low and simmer 10 minutes. Add the brown rice syrup and shoyu, reduce the heat to low, and simmer another 10 minutes. Drain the shiitake and set aside.

2. While the shiitake are simmering, cut the avocado into slices and place in a small bowl. Sprinkle with lemon juice to prevent discoloration.

3. Place a sheet of nori (smooth, shiny side down) on a sushi mat. Spread one-fourth of the rice on the nori, leaving a 1-inch border at the bottom and a 2-inch border at the top. Flatten the rice firmly with a slightly wet bamboo rice paddle or wooden spatula.

4. Place a row of shiitake lengthwise across the center of the rice. Next, place a row of avocado slices, then a row of ginger slices. Sprinkle the rice with furikake.

5. Lightly moisten the top border of the nori with water, then, starting at the bottom, roll up the nori using the sushi mat. Press gently but firmly while rolling.

6. Continue making rolls with the remaining nori and filling. If you are not serving the sushi right away, place the uncut rolls on a platter, cover with plastic wrap, and refrigerate. This will prevent the rolls from drying out.

7. Just before serving, place a roll on a cutting surface, lightly moisten a sharp knife, and slice the roll in half. Moisten the knife slightly again, and cut each half in half. Once again, moisten the knife, and slice each quarter in half. This will yield 8 pieces.

8. Serve the rounds plain or with the recommended accompaniments.

Yield: 4 sushi rolls (32 pieces)

1 cup dried shiitake mushroom slices

1 cup water

2 tablespoons brown rice syrup or maple syrup

1 tablespoon shoyu soy sauce

2 avocados

1 tablespoon fresh lemon juice

4 sheets toasted nori

1 recipe Sushi Rice (page 90), at room temperature

4-ounce package pickled ginger slices, drained

$^1/_3$ cup Sushi Furikake (page 66) or toasted sesame seeds

GARNISH OPTIONS

Wasabi paste

Pickled ginger slices

Shoyu soy sauce

Wasabi-Shoyu Dipping Sauce (page 62)

California Rolls

Most sushi rolls have nori on the outside. For California rolls, the nori is covered with sticky rice that is typically coated with toasted sesame seeds. These "reverse sushi rolls" are usually filled with avocado, cucumber, and cooked crabmeat. This recipe offers a delicious vegetarian version.

**Yield: 4 sushi rolls
(32 pieces)**

2 avocados

1 tablespoon fresh lemon juice

1 recipe Sushi Rice (page 90),
at room temperature

4 sheets toasted nori

4-ounce package pickled ginger
slices, drained

$^1/_2$ cup toasted sesame seeds
or Gomashio (page 67)

GARNISH OPTIONS

Wasabi paste

Pickled ginger slices

Shoyu soy sauce

Wasabi-Shoyu Dipping Sauce
(page 62)

1. Cut the avocado into slices and place in a small bowl. Sprinkle with lemon juice to prevent discoloration.

2. Place a sheet of nori (smooth, shiny side down) on a sushi mat. Spread about one-fourth of the rice on the nori, leaving a 1-inch border at the bottom and 2-inch border at the top. Flatten the rice firmly with a slightly wet bamboo rice paddle or wooden spatula.

3. Sprinkle one-fourth of the sesame seeds evenly over the rice. Cover the rice with a sheet of plastic wrap, place another sushi mat on top, then flip the mats over. Remove the top mat.

4. Place a row of avocado strips and ginger slices lengthwise across the center of the nori.

5. Lightly moisten the top border of the nori with water, then, starting at the bottom, roll up the nori using the sushi mat. Pull the plastic wrap away as you roll, and press gently to keep the roll firm.

6. Continue making rolls with the remaining nori and filling. If you are not serving the sushi right away, place the uncut rolls on a platter, cover with plastic wrap, and refrigerate. This will prevent the rolls from drying out.

7. Just before serving, place a roll on a cutting surface, lightly moisten a sharp knife, and slice the roll in half. Moisten the knife slightly again, and cut each half in half. Once again, moisten the knife, and slice each quarter in half. This will yield 8 pieces.

8. Arrange the rounds on a platter and serve plain or with the recommended garnishes.

6

Simple Sides

Brown rice is an extremely versatile grain. Satisfying and delicious in its simple unadorned state, this hearty grain also partners perfectly with other whole grains and beans. In this chapter, you'll find a wide selection of basic brown rice side dishes that are fairly straightforward and uncomplicated. Most are rice-and-grain or rice-and-bean combinations that you can enjoy plain or crowned with your favorite sauce or gravy.

Although I consider these dishes to be on the simple side, they are far from tasteless or boring. The addition of ingredients like nuts, seeds, dried fruit, mushrooms, and/or vegetables further increases their flavor, as well as their texture and nutritional value. Dishes like the Wild Mushroom Rice, Pecan Rice, and Coconut Rice never fail to garner compli-

ments. Equally pleasing are the Baked Rice Casserole and the Vegetable Fried Rice.

The flavorful Rice 'n Bread Stuffing is my family's traditional Thanksgiving favorite. We enjoy it so much, I find myself making it often throughout the year. Another family winner is the Mock Mashed Potatoes—a creamy blend of brown rice, millet, and cauliflower. It is a satisfying whole grain alternative to traditional mashed potatoes. Among my personal favorites in this chapter is the Azuki Bean Rice. I always make plenty, so I can fry up the leftovers to enjoy the next day. And as a tribute to my love for all things Japanese, there is a recipe for Gomoku—a mixed rice dish that is the equivalent of Spanish paella.

Once you have tried the side dishes in this chapter, I'm hoping you will make them a regular part of your healthy diet. Enjoy!

Basic Brown Rice and Soft Grains

Yield: 4 to 6 servings

1 ¹/₂ cups short-, medium-, or long-grain brown rice, rinsed and drained

¹/₂ cup amaranth, buckwheat, millet, quinoa, teff, partially pearled barley, or wild rice, rinsed and drained

4 cups cold water

1 pinch sea salt

The relatively quick-cooking soft grains listed in this recipe do not require soaking, and they can be cooked right along with the brown rice. For more information, see the inset below.

1. Place all of the ingredients in a heavy medium-size pot and bring to a boil over high heat. Reduce the heat to medium-low, stir once, and cover. Simmer 45 to 50 minutes or until the liquid is absorbed and the grains are tender.

2. Remove from the heat and let sit for 10 minutes. Transfer to a bowl and serve.

COOKING BROWN RICE WITH OTHER GRAINS

A simple dish of brown rice, flavored with a splash of soy sauce, a sprinkle of sesame seeds, or a spoonful or two of your favorite gravy, makes a nutritious, satisfying side. One way to elevate this basic dish even further is to combine the rice with other grains for added texture, flavor, and even visual interest.

Many grains, including amaranth, buckwheat, millet, quinoa, teff, partially pearled barley, and wild rice, are relatively quick cooking. Without being presoaked or parboiled, these softer grains can be cooked right along with the rice, as seen in the basic recipe above.

Harder, longer-cooking whole grains, such as wheat (including hard red spring, hard red winter,

white pastry, Kamut, and spelt), barley, oats, and rye, require six to eight hours of soaking before they can be cooked together with rice. Pressure cooking is recommended for this, as shown in the recipe for Basic Brown Rice and Hard Grains on page 103. These harder grains can also be prepared separately and then simply added to rice that is already cooked.

When preparing these combination dishes, I find the best rice-to-grain proportion to be 3 parts rice to 1 part of the other grain. Every cup of this uncooked combination will yield around 2¹/₂ to 3 cups cooked.

Brown Rice & Barley with Mushrooms

Barley adds lightness and a pleasant chewy texture to this dish, while savory mushrooms complement the mild sweetness of the grains. For this recipe, I prefer dried mushrooms over fresh, as I find their flavor to be more earthy and complex. As an added bonus, the soaking water, which is infused with flavor, can be used as part of the cooking liquid.

1. Place the shiitake in a small bowl, cover with $1/2$ cup warm water, and let soak 15 to 20 minutes or until soft. Reserving the soaking water, remove the shiitake and coarsely chop. (If using whole shiitake, remove and discard the stems.)

2. Transfer the shiitake and soaking water to a heavy medium-size pot. Add all of the remaining ingredients and bring to a boil over high heat. Reduce the heat to medium-low, stir once, and cover. Simmer 45 to 50 minutes or until the liquid is absorbed and the grains are tender.

3. Remove from the heat and let sit for 10 minutes. Transfer to a bowl and serve.

Yield: 4 to 6 servings

$1/3$ cup dried shiitake mushrooms

$1/2$ cup warm water
for soaking shiitake

$1 1/2$ cups short-, medium-,
or long-grain brown rice,
rinsed and drained

$1/2$ cup partially pearled barley,
rinsed and drained

$3 1/2$ cups cold water

1 pinch sea salt

FOR A CHANGE . . .

- Instead of or in combination with shiitake, try any dried mushroom variety. Maitake, matsutake, black trumpet, portabella, porcini, crimini, chanterelle, oyster, wood ear, forest mix, and morels are all good choices.

- For increased flavor and texture, add $1/4$ cup fresh or frozen sweet corn in Step 2.

- Once the grains are cooked, mix in some cooked green peas for added flavor and color.

Multi-Grain Combo

*Combining brown rice with a variety of other grains in this
dish results in multiple flavors, textures, and colors.
Add leftovers to soups and stews, or use in whole
grain salads, burgers, or croquettes.*

Yield: 4 to 6 servings

1 1/4 cups short-, medium-,
or long-grain brown rice,
rinsed and drained

1/4 cup red or black rice,
rinsed and drained

1/4 cup wild rice,
rinsed and drained*

1/4 cup partially pearled barley,
rinsed and drained

4 cups cold water

1 pinch sea salt

* Native American hand-harvested wild
rice is preferred (see page 130).

1. Place all of the ingredients in a heavy medium-size pot
and bring to a boil over high heat. Reduce the heat to
medium-low, stir once, and cover. Simmer 45 to 50 minutes
or until the liquid is absorbed and the grains are tender.

2. Remove from the heat and let sit for 10 minutes. Transfer to a bowl and serve.

FOR A CHANGE . . .

● Be creative and try other multi-grain combinations to cook
with the brown rice in this recipe. Amaranth, buckwheat, millet, quinoa, and teff are also good choices.

Basic Brown Rice and Hard Grains

As explained in the inset on page 100, hard whole grains need to be soaked before they are cooked together with brown rice. I find pressure-cooking to be the best method for this combination—it takes less time to cook than boiling, and you can soak the grains directly in the cooker. In this recipe, the water-to-grain ratio and cooking time are fairly standard; however, some pressure cookers may have slightly different instructions. Follow your cooker's directions for best results.

1. Place the rice, wheat (or other grain), and water in a pressure cooker. Place the lid on, but do not seal. Let soak 6 to 8 hours or overnight.

2. Once the grains are soaked, add the salt and secure the lid on the cooker. Place on the stovetop over high heat and bring up to full pressure (according to the operating manual). Reduce the heat to low and cook 45 to 50 minutes (or as instructed in the manual).

3. Remove the cooker from the heat and let the pressure come down on its own (about 5 to 10 minutes).

4. Remove the cover, spoon the cooked grains into a bowl, and serve.

Yield: 4 to 6 servings

1 $\frac{1}{2}$ cups short-, medium-, or long-grain brown rice, rinsed and drained

$\frac{1}{2}$ cup whole wheat, Kamut, spelt, barley, oats, or rye, rinsed and drained

3 cups cold water

1 pinch sea salt

A Little Rice Trivia . . .

Rice and its byproducts are used in the production of many nonfood items, including packing filler, straw, rope, paper, and cosmetics. Rice straw is often woven and used to make handbags, totes, hats, and even sandals.

Baked Rice Casserole

Containing almonds, dried cranberries, and both brown and wild rice, this delicious casserole is especially nice when the weather is cold and you don't mind using the oven. Dry roasting the rice before baking gives the dish a light fluffy quality. Leftovers make delicious stuffing !

Yield: 4 to 6 servings

1 cup short-, medium-, or
long-grain brown rice,
rinsed and drained

1 cup wild rice, rinsed and drained*

6 cups boiling water

1/2 cup blanched raw almonds,
skins removed

1/2 cup dried cranberries

1 teaspoon ground sage
or poultry seasoning

1 pinch sea salt

1/4 cup minced fresh parsley

* Native American hand-harvested
wild rice is preferred (see page 130).

1. Preheat the oven to 350°F. Lightly coat a 13-x-9-inch baking dish with cooking oil and set aside.

2. Combine the brown and wild rice in a heavy medium-size skillet over medium-low heat. Stirring occasionally, dry roast the rice for 5 to 7 minutes or until it releases a nutty aroma and turns slightly golden.

3. Transfer the roasted rice to the prepared baking dish. Add all of the remaining ingredients except the parsley and mix well. Cover the dish with foil or a tight-fitting lid. Bake for 1 hour or until the liquid is absorbed and the rice is tender and fluffy.

4. Stir the parsley into the baked casserole. Serve hot.

FOR A CHANGE . . .

● Instead of almonds, add coarsely chopped roasted pecans or walnuts in Step 4.

● Add 1/4 cup sautéed diced onions, celery, and mushrooms to the rice mixture before baking.

● Substitute red rice for the wild rice.

● In place of dried cranberries, use dried blueberries or coarsely chopped dried cherries or apricots.

Rice 'n Bread Stuffing

My all-time favorite dish on Thanksgiving has always been this healthy, flavorful stuffing—and it still is. But I don't serve it only on Thanksgiving. My family and I enjoy this delicious side dish all year long.

1. Preheat the oven to 350° F. Lightly coat an 8-x-10-inch baking dish with cooking oil and set aside.

2. Heat the oil in a medium skillet over medium heat. Add the onion, and sauté for 3 to 4 minutes or until beginning to soften. Add the mushrooms and soy sauce, and sauté another 3 to 5 minutes or until the mushrooms have released their juice. Add the celery, and continue to sauté for 1 to 2 minutes.

3. While the vegetables are sautéing, place the bread and rice in a large mixing bowl. Add the sautéed vegetables, stock, sage, and poultry seasoning. Toss well.

4. Add the mixture to the prepared baking dish, cover, and bake for 25 to 30 minutes. Uncover and bake another 10 minutes to brown the top. Serve hot.

FOR A CHANGE . . .

- Instead of all brown rice, use any rice and grain combination. Brown rice and wild rice make a great combo (and a family favorite in my home).
- For a richer flavor, use only 1 cup of stock, and add 1 cup plain unsweetened soymilk.
- For a bit of sweetness and added texture, include ¼ cup dried cranberries and ¼ cup chopped roasted walnuts or pecans to the stuffing mixture before baking.

Yield: 6 to 8 servings

2 tablespoons extra virgin olive or safflower oil

1 cup diced onion

1 cup diced button mushrooms

2 teaspoons shoyu soy sauce, or ½ teaspoon sea salt

½ cup diced celery

8 cups cubed day-old whole wheat bread

3 cups cooked short-, medium-, or long-grain brown rice (page 19)

2 cups Mushroom Stock (page 49) or commercial variety

1 teaspoon ground sage

1 teaspoon poultry seasoning

Mock Mashed Potatoes

*Always a hit, this creamy blend of brown rice, millet,
and cauliflower makes a satisfying whole grain
alternative to mashed potatoes.*

Yield: 4 to 6 servings

1 1/2 cups millet, rinsed and drained

1 cup cooked short-, medium-, or
long-grain brown rice (page 19)

1 medium cauliflower,
cut into florets

4 cups cold water

1 pinch sea salt

Mushroom Gravy (page 71),
or commercial variety

Minced fresh parsley for garnish

1. Place the millet, rice, cauliflower, water, and salt in a
heavy medium-size pot. Cover and bring to a boil over
high heat.

2. Reduce the heat to medium-low, and simmer for 30 to
35 minutes or until the liquid is absorbed, the grains are
tender, and the cauliflower is soft. Remove from the heat
and let sit 10 minutes.

3. Using a potato masher or hand-held blender, mash the
ingredients right in the pot until they become the consistency of mashed potatoes.

4. Enjoy topped with gravy and a sprinkling of parsley.

Fried Azuki Bean Rice

*Sometimes I think I make Azuki Bean Rice just so I will have
leftovers for this dish . . . one of my all-time favorites.*

Yield: 4 to 6 servings

1 tablespoon extra virgin olive oil

1 tablespoon toasted or
plain sesame oil

4 cups cooked Azuki Bean Rice
(page 113)

1 tablespoon shoyu soy sauce,
or 1/2 teaspoon sea salt

1/2 cup finely chopped scallions

1. Heat the oils in a medium skillet over medium-high
heat. Add the rice and shoyu, and fry, stirring frequently,
for 5 to 7 minutes or until the rice is hot.

2. Add the scallions, and continue to fry another 3 minutes or until the scallions are bright green and tender.

3. Transfer to a serving bowl and enjoy hot.

Gomoku
Mixed Rice

This popular Japanese mixed rice dish typically includes five or more ingredients (gomoku actually translates as "five variety"). It is the Japanese equivalent of Spanish paella.

1. Place the shiitake in a small bowl, cover with the warm water, and let soak 15 to 20 minutes or until soft. Reserving the soaking water, remove the shiitake and coarsely chop.

2. Transfer the shiitake and soaking water to a heavy medium-size pot. Add all of the remaining ingredients except the edamame and bring to a boil over high heat.

3. Reduce the heat to medium-low, stir once, and cover. Simmer 45 to 50 minutes or until the liquid is absorbed and the rice is tender.

4. Remove from the heat and let sit 10 minutes.

5. Transfer the gomoku to a serving bowl, top with edamame, and serve.

FOR A CHANGE . . .

- For added saltiness, simmer the deep-fried tofu in 1 cup water with 2 teaspoons shoyu soy sauce for 10 minutes before adding to the pot.
- Substitute seitan or tempeh cubes for the tofu.
- Instead of all shiitake, use any variety or combination of dried mushrooms.
- For added crunch, toss in a handful of roasted nuts at the end of cooking time.
- Instead of fresh ginger, add minced pickled ginger slices at the end of cooking time.
- Try other vegetables with this dish. Burdock and fresh or dried lotus root are recommended.

Yield: 4 to 6 servings

$1/_3$ cup dried shiitake mushroom slices

1 cup warm water for soaking shiitake

2 cups short-, medium-, or long-grain brown rice, rinsed and drained

3 cups cold water

1 cup deep-fried tofu cubes

$1/_2$ cup fresh or frozen sweet corn

$1/_2$ cup diced carrots

$1/_3$ cup diced daikon radish, rutabaga, or turnips

$1/_4$ cup diced celery

1 tablespoon minced ginger

1 pinch sea salt

1 cup blanched shelled edamame

Wild Mushroom Rice

This delicious dish gets its fluffy texture from long-grain basmati and protein-rich wild rice, and its earthy flavor from a blend of dried mushrooms.

Yield: 4 to 6 servings

1/2 cup dried shiitake mushroom slices

1/4 cup dried porcini mushrooms

1/4 cup dried crimini mushrooms

3 1/4 cups water (including mushroom soaking water)

1 cup brown basmati rice or long-grain brown rice, rinsed and drained

1/2 cup wild rice, rinsed and drained*

1/4 cup fresh orange juice

1 pinch sea salt

1/2 cup blanched diced carrots

1/4 cup blanched fresh or frozen green peas

1/3 cup coarsely chopped roasted pecans, walnuts, and/or hazelnuts

Finely chopped chives for garnish

* Native American hand-harvested wild rice is preferred (see page 130).

1. Place all of the mushrooms in a medium bowl and cover with warm water. Soak for 10 minutes or until soft, then coarsely chop.

2. Pour the soaking water into a measuring cup, then add enough cold water to equal 3 1/4 cups. Place in a heavy medium-size pot along with the mushrooms, orange juice, and salt. Bring to a boil over high heat.

3. Add the rice to the pot. Reduce the heat to medium-low, stir once, and cover. Simmer for 45 to 50 minutes or until the liquid is absorbed and the rice is tender. Remove from the heat and let sit for 10 minutes

4. Add the carrots, peas, and nuts to the rice, and gently stir until well combined.

5. Transfer the mixture to a serving bowl, garnish with chives, and enjoy!

Vegetable Fried Rice

Deliciously rich and satisfying, this dish is the perfect choice when leftover brown rice is on hand. You can use just about any type of brown rice—alone or in combination with other leftover grains—and the vegetable choices are endless.

1. Heat the oil in a large skillet over high heat. Add the onion, and sauté 2 to 3 minutes or until beginning to soften. Add the bell pepper and corn, and continue to sauté another 2 to 3 minutes.

2. Reduce the heat to medium, and add the rice and shoyu to the skillet. Stir the mixture frequently for 5 to 7 minutes or until the vegetables are cooked and the rice is piping hot.

3. Transfer the rice to a serving bowl, sprinkle with chives, and serve.

FOR A CHANGE . . .

- Toss in a handful or two of cooked beans for added protein, flavor, and texture. Black beans, pinto, and chickpeas are popular choices.
- For a different, more intense flavor, use half olive oil and half toasted sesame oil.
- Sauté a minced garlic clove with the onion in Step 1.

Yield: 4 to 5 servings

2 tablespoons extra virgin olive oil

$1/2$ cup diced onion or shallot

$1/4$ cup diced red bell pepper

$1/4$ cup fresh or frozen sweet corn

4 to 5 cups cooked brown rice, any variety (see page 19)

1 tablespoon shoyu soy sauce, or $1/2$ teaspoon sea salt

Minced fresh chives or finely chopped scallions for garnish

A Little Rice Trivia . . .

All rice is gluten free; in addition, it is the most non-allergenic of all cereal grains.

Pecan Rice

Although traditional Louisiana pecan rice is made with beef broth, I prefer low-fat mushroom stock—a healthier choice.

Yield: 4 to 6 servings

3 tablespoons extra virgin olive oil

I medium onion, diced

$^1/_4$ cup finely chopped celery

I clove garlic, finely chopped

2 cups long-grain brown basmati rice, rinsed and drained

4 cups Mushroom Stock (page 49), or commercial variety

I pinch sea salt

I cup toasted pecan pieces

$^1/_2$ cup minced fresh parsley

$^1/_2$ cup chopped scallions

1. Heat the oil in a heavy medium-size pot over medium-low heat. Add the onions, celery, and garlic, and sauté 3 to 5 minutes or until beginning to soften.

2. Add the rice, stock, and salt to the pot, increase the heat to high, and bring to a boil.

3. Reduce the heat to medium-low, stir once, and cover. Simmer for 30 to 35 minutes or until the liquid is absorbed and the rice is tender. Add the pecans and cook another 10 minutes.

4. Remove from the heat and let sit for 10 minutes.

5. Add the parsley and scallions to the rice, and gently mix to combine. Transfer to a serving bowl and enjoy.

FOR A CHANGE . . .

● For a spicier version, add a tablespoon of Cajun seasoning and/or 1 teaspoon of your favorite hot sauce.

● Instead of basmati, use Texmati, Della, or wild pecan rice. The liquid may need a slight adjustment, so be sure to follow package directions or the cooking instructions on page 19.

Almond Rice

*Combining nuts with brown rice results
in a complete-protein dish.*

1. Place all of the ingredients in a heavy medium-size pot, and bring to a boil over high heat.

2. Reduce the heat to medium-low, stir once, and cover. Simmer for 45 to 50 minutes or until the liquid is absorbed and the rice is tender.

3. Remove from the heat and let sit for 10 minutes. Transfer to a serving bowl and enjoy hot.

Yield: 4 to 6 servings

2 cups short-, medium-, or long-grain brown rice, rinsed and drained

$1/2$ cup blanched slivered almonds

4 cups water

1 pinch sea salt

FOR A CHANGE . . .

- Before serving, add a sprinkle of Gomashio (page 67) for extra flavor and nutrients.

- Serve topped with your favorite sauce or gravy. Mushroom Gravy (page 71) and Mushroom-Onion Sauce (page 70) are good choices.

Rice is nice . . .
to help soothe sore, aching muscles.

Instead of a heating pad, dry roast some rice in a heavy skillet, then add the hot grains to a cloth bag or sock. Place the heated bag against sore muscles— lay it over your shoulders, against your back, or around your neck. You can even use it to keep your feet warm on cold winter nights! It is best to use a thick sock or bag so the grains don't poke through. As an alternative, you can pop it in the microwave for a few seconds.

Coconut Rice

This dish goes especially well with Southeast Asian, Indian, and Caribbean-style dishes. It's simple to make and absolutely delicious.

Yield: 4 to 6 servings

1 tablespoon peanut or
extra virgin olive oil

1 tablespoon minced fresh ginger

2 small cloves garlic, minced

6-inch cinnamon stick, or
$1/4$ teaspoon ground cinnamon

2 cups brown jasmine rice,
rinsed and drained

2 cups coconut milk

2 cups cold water

$1/2$ teaspoon grated lime zest

$1/4$ teaspoon sea salt

$1/4$ teaspoon white pepper

Shredded unsweetened coconut
for garnish

1. Heat the oil in a heavy medium-size pot over medium heat. Add the ginger, garlic, and cinnamon stick, and sauté for 1 to 2 minutes or until fragrant.

2. Add the rice and sauté another 2 to 3 minutes. Increase the heat to high, add all of the remaining ingredients except the shredded coconut, and bring to a boil.

3. Reduce the heat to medium-low, stir once, and cover. Simmer for 35 to 45 minutes or until the liquid is absorbed and the rice is tender.

4. While the rice is cooking, toast the coconut in a dry skillet over low heat until slightly golden brown. Remove and set aside.

5. When the rice is done, remove the pot from the heat. Fluff with a fork, and let rest for 5 minutes.

6. Transfer the rice to a serving dish, top with toasted coconut, and serve.

FOR A CHANGE . . .

• For added visual appeal, toss in $1/2$ cup blanched green peas or edamame just before serving.

• Try using white jasmine rice instead of brown. Reduce both the coconut milk and water to $1^1/2$ cups, and reduce the cooking time to 15 to 20 minutes.

• Add 1 teaspoon honey to the rice as it simmers in Step 2.

Azuki Bean Rice

This dish, often referred to as "red rice" in Japan, gets its color from azuki beans. I find parboiling the beans and then using the cooking liquid as part of the water measurement gives this dish the deepest red color.

1. Place the azuki beans and 3 cups of water in a heavy medium-size pot over high heat, and bring to a boil. Reduce the heat to medium-low, and simmer 1 hour or until partially cooked.

2. Reserving the cooking liquid, drain the beans and return to the pot. Add enough water to the cooking liquid to measure 4 cups, then add to the pot along with the rice and salt.

3. Bring the ingredients to a boil over high heat. Reduce the heat to medium-low, stir once, and cover. Simmer for 45 to 50 minutes or until the liquid is absorbed, the rice is tender, and the beans are cooked.

4. Remove from the heat and let sit for 10 minutes. Transfer to a serving bowl and enjoy hot.

Yield: 4 to 6 servings

1 cup azuki beans,
rinsed and drained

3 cups cold water for
cooking azuki

2 cups short-, medium-,
or long-grain brown rice,
rinsed and drained

4 cups cold water (including
the azuki cooking water)

1 pinch sea salt

FOR A CHANGE . . .

- For a quicker version, instead of dried beans, add a 15-ounce can cooked azukis to the rice in Step 3. Drain the beans and use the canned liquid as part of the water measurement. When using canned azukis, be aware that the flavor of the dish won't be as strong and the color won't be as brilliant.

- If you have any leftovers, be sure to try the Fried Azuki Bean Rice on page 106.

Black Soybean Rice

Pressure-cooking is the preferred method for this dish, which is very popular in Japan. It is always served at festive occasions, especially when celebrating the New Year.

Yield: 4 to 6 servings

I cup dried black soybeans, rinsed and drained*

2 cups short-grain brown rice, rinsed and drained

4¹/₂ cups water

I pinch sea salt

* Hokkaido black soybeans are recommended.

1. Place the soybeans in a heavy medium-size skillet over medium heat. Stirring constantly, dry roast the beans about 3 to 5 minutes or until the skins become tight and split slightly. *Do not over-roast or the beans will scorch and become bitter.*

2. Transfer the beans to a pressure cooker along with the rice, water, and salt. Place on the stovetop over high heat and bring up to full pressure (according to the operating manual). Reduce the heat to medium-low, and cook 40 to 45 minutes.

3. Remove the cooker from the heat and let the pressure come down on its own (about 5 to 10 minutes).

4. Remove the cover, spoon the rice into a bowl, and serve.

FOR A CHANGE . . .

• If you do not have a pressure cooker, simply add a 15-ounce can black soybeans (rinsed and drained) to 2 cups freshly cooked boiled brown rice.

A Little Rice Trivia . . .

Throughout Asia, rice-planting festivals are held between May and June, while rice-harvesting festivals take place in the fall. In the United States, annual festivals celebrating this grain are held after the harvest in Louisiana, Arkansas, Texas, California, and other rice-producing states.

7

Specialty Sides

Did you know that expanding your dietary choices and varying the foods you eat not only keeps your meals interesting, but also may be good for your heart?

The Framingham Heart Study, the nation's oldest continuous heart research project, conducted a survey of the eating habits of the people living in Framingham, Massachusetts—considered an average American city. The results showed that the average American family has a repertoire of about ten main dishes, which are prepared and served weekly, often on the same day of the week. Very seldom did this deviate from the norm. The study concluded that this lack of variety or change in eating habits may actually be a contributing factor in heart disease.

Just as the seasons change, so should our eating habits. Serving the same dishes week after week will inevitably become a little ho-hum. In my family, especially when the children were young, one night a week was reserved for an international dinner. Everyone was excited about these special meals, which expanded our awareness of the foods, customs, and traditions from around the world.

In this chapter, I have included some of the specialty side dishes enjoyed at those dinners, and others that I created for my cooking classes. Starting out, you'll find a beautiful selection of creamy risottos. The first time I made risotto with brown rice rather than traditional Arborio, I fell in love with how sweet and creamy it was. The Native American Wild Rice and the Moroccan Rice are other stellar choices, as are the Mediterranean Rice Pilaf and the Baked Herbed Rice and Lentils. The choices go on and on. I hope you try them all!

Fresh Mushroom Risotto

This mouthwatering dish is rich with the earthiness of savory mushrooms. A hint of lemon adds the perfect spark of flavor.

Yield: 4 to 6 servings

5 cups Mushroom Stock (page 49) or commercial variety

5 tablespoons extra virgin olive oil, divided

2¹/₂ cups sliced fresh porcini mushrooms

¹/₂ cup finely chopped onions

¹/₄ cup finely chopped shallots

2 cloves garlic, minced

I teaspoon sea salt, or to taste

¹/₄ teaspoon black pepper, or to taste

I cup short-grain brown rice, rinsed and drained

¹/₄ cup finely chopped parsley

2 tablespoons minced fresh celery leaves

2 teaspoons fresh lemon juice

I teaspoon dried sage

¹/₂ teaspoon lemon zest

1. Bring the stock to a boil in a medium pot. Reduce the heat to low to keep it hot.

2. Heat 2 tablespoons of the oil in a medium skillet over medium-low heat. Add the mushrooms, onions, shallots, and garlic, and sauté 3 to 5 minutes or until the mushrooms release their juice. Add half the salt and pepper, and sauté another 2 to 3 minutes. Set aside.

3. Heat the remaining oil in a heavy medium-size pot over medium-high heat. Add the rice and stir well to coat the grains with oil.

4. Reduce the heat to medium and add about 1 cup of the hot stock to the rice. Stir frequently for about 12 minutes or until the rice has absorbed most of the stock. Continue adding stock 1 cup at a time and stirring until all (or most) has been added and the rice is tender but firm. This should take around 50 to 55 minutes.

5. Add the sautéed mushroom-onion mixture and all of the remaining ingredients to the rice. Stir well, reduce the heat to low, and continue to cook another 5 to 7 minutes or until thick and creamy.

6. Serve piping hot.

FOR A CHANGE . . .

- Use different fresh mushroom combinations. Chanterelles, crimini, shiitake, and portabella are all flavorful choices.

- Add 1 cup fresh or frozen green peas during the last few minutes of cooking for added color and sweetness.

- For added flavor, first add ¹/₂ cup dry white wine to the rice in Step 4. Once it is absorbed, continue with the stock.

- Substitute white Arborio rice for the brown. Arborio does not need to be rinsed. It will also absorb the stock more quickly than brown rice (about 20 to 25 minutes), which is why it needs to be stirred constantly. (Brown rice must be stirred *frequently*, but not *constantly*.) Arborio also requires about 1 cup less stock for this recipe.

Quick 'n Easy
Brown Rice Risotto

Here's an even quicker risotto version. It may not win any awards from your traditional-minded Italian grandmother, but it's an easy, delicious option when there's no time to cook. It calls for canned brown rice and chickpeas, which is available in most natural foods stores and large supermarkets.

1. Place the shiitake, maitake, and water in a small pot and bring to a boil over high heat. Cover, reduce the heat to medium-low, and simmer 8 to 10 minutes or until most of the water has evaporated and the mushrooms are tender. Coarsely chop the mushrooms and set aside.

2. Heat the oil in a medium pot over medium-low heat. Add the onion, shallot, and garlic, and sauté for 3 to 4 minutes or until beginning to soften.

3. Add the canned rice and chickpeas, mushrooms, roasted red pepper, salt, and black pepper. Increase the heat to medium, cover, and cook 2 to 3 minutes or until heated through.

4. Stir the peas and basil into the mixture, and cook another 2 to 3 minutes. Serve piping hot.

Yield: 4 to 6 servings

$1/2$ cup dried shiitake mushroom slices

$1/2$ cup dried maitake mushrooms

1 cup water

1 tablespoon extra virgin olive oil

$1/2$ cup finely diced onion

$1/4$ cup finely diced shallot

1 clove garlic, finely minced

2 cans (15-ounces each) brown rice and chickpeas

$1/4$ cup finely chopped roasted red pepper

$1/8$ teaspoon sea salt

$1/8$ teaspoon black pepper

$1/2$ cup fresh or frozen green peas

1 teaspoon minced fresh basil

Golden Risotto

Cooking naturally sweet-tasting pumpkin or butternut squash with creamy short-grain brown rice results in the perfect comfort food. And its golden-orange sunshine color is sure to brighten your day.

Yield: 4 to 6 servings

2 cups Vegetable Stock (page 48) or commercial variety

4 cups cubed ($^1/_2$-inch) sugar baby pumpkin or butternut squash

$2^1/_2$ cups water

3 tablespoons extra virgin olive oil

1 small onion or shallot, minced

1 clove garlic, minced

1 cup short-grain brown rice, rinsed and drained

$^1/_2$ cup dry white wine

1 teaspoon sea salt

$^1/_4$ teaspoon black pepper

$^1/_4$ cup chopped fresh parsley

1. Bring the stock to a boil in a medium pot. Reduce the heat to low to keep it hot.

2. Place the pumpkin and water in a medium pot, cover, and bring to a boil over high heat. Reduce the heat to medium-low, and simmer for 4 to 5 minutes or until the pumpkin is tender. Remove from the heat and let sit for 3 to 5 minutes.

3. Remove half the pumpkin with a slotted spoon and set aside. Transfer the remaining pumpkin and cooking water to a blender, and purée several seconds until creamy.

4. Heat the oil in a heavy 4-quart pot over medium heat. Add the onion and garlic, and sauté for 3 to 5 minutes or until translucent. Add the rice, stirring constantly until slightly toasted but not brown.

5. Reduce the heat to medium-low and add the wine to the rice. Stirring frequently, cook for about 5 to 7 minutes or until the rice has absorbed most of the wine. Continuing to stir, add 1 cup of the puréed pumpkin, and cook for about 12 minutes or until it is absorbed by the rice.

6. Continue adding the puréed pumpkin and the hot vegetable stock to the rice 1 cup at a time, making sure each cup is absorbed before adding the next. Continue until all (or most) of the liquid has been added and the rice is creamy and tender yet firm. This will take about 50 to 55 minutes.

7. Gently stir the reserved pumpkin cubes into the cooked rice. Add the salt and pepper, reduce the heat to low, and simmer for 5 to 7 minutes or until thick and creamy.

8. Gently stir the parsley into the risotto and serve.

FOR A CHANGE . . .

- Use any variety of pumpkin or winter squash for this recipe except acorn squash—the skin is too tough.
- For added flavor, include $1/2$ teaspoon dried sage at the end of cooking.
- Top each serving with a dash of cinnamon and some chopped toasted walnuts, pecans, hazelnuts, or slivered almonds.

RISOTTO . . .
COMFORT FOOD SUPREME!

Warm and filling, creamy risotto is the Italian equivalent of Japanese Okayu (page 28). It is traditionally made with white Arborio or carnaroli rice, which are known for their creaminess, but short-grain brown rice also works well.

One of the keys to making great risotto is lots of stirring, stirring, stirring while s-l-o-w-l-y adding liquid to the rice as it cooks.

Although this dish requires a fair amount of attention, it is easy to prepare, requires only one pot, and offers delectable results. In other words, any effort put forth will be rewarded. And although the risotto recipes in this chapter are made without the butter and parmesan cheese found in classic versions, they are just as satisfying and delicious (and healthier, too).

On a personal note, the first time I made risotto with brown rice rather than Arborio, it immediately became my new favorite. The rice is creamy and sweet and absolutely delicious. It does take a little longer to cook—brown rice doesn't absorb the liquid as quickly as Arborio—but on the plus side, for this same reason, it doesn't require constant stirring. (It *does* need to be stirred frequently, but not constantly.) Best of all, I prefer the way it tastes. I'm betting you will, too.

Oven-Baked Mushroom Risotto

Here's an easy, less attention-needy version of risotto that's oven baked (and just as delicious).

Yield: 4 to 6 servings

1½ cups dried shiitake mushroom slices

1 cup warm water for soaking mushrooms

5 tablespoons extra virgin olive oil

2 cups sliced fresh crimini, porcini, chanterelle, and/or portabella mushrooms

½ cup finely chopped onions or shallots

2 cloves garlic, minced

5 cups Mushroom Stock (page 49) or commercial variety

1 cup short-grain brown rice, rinsed and drained

1 teaspoon sea salt, or to taste

¼ teaspoon black pepper, or to taste

1 cup fresh or frozen green peas

1. Preheat the oven to 350°F. Place the shiitake in a small bowl, cover with the warm water, and let soak 15 to 20 minutes or until soft. Reserving the soaking water, remove the softened mushrooms and set aside.

2. Heat the oil in a medium Dutch oven or 4-quart oven-proof pot with a tight fitting lid. Add the mushrooms, onions, and garlic, and sauté for 3 to 5 minutes or until the onions are soft and translucent.

3. Add the mushroom soaking water to the stock. Reserving 1 cup, add the remaining liquid to the pot and bring to a boil. Stir in the rice, salt, and pepper.

4. Cover the pot and transfer to the oven. Stirring occasionally, bake for 45 to 50 minutes or until most of the liquid is absorbed and the rice is nearly cooked, yet firm.

5. Return the pot to the stovetop over medium-low heat and uncover. Stir ½ cup of the reserved stock into the rice. Stirring occasionally, cook for 5 to 7 minutes or until tender and creamy.

6. Add the remaining stock and peas to the rice, and cook another 5 to 7 minutes or until the peas are bright green. Serve immediately.

FOR A CHANGE . . .

- Substitute other dried mushroom varieties for the shiitake.
- Add ½ cup dry white wine to the rice along with the reserved stock in Step 5.

Green Pea Risotto

*Sweet-flavored green pea risotto is a springtime favorite
in Italy. Although it is best made with fresh peas,
you can also use frozen with delicious results.*

1. Bring the stock to boil in a medium pot. Reduce the heat to low to keep it hot.

2. Heat the oil in a heavy medium-size pot over medium-high heat. Add the onion, shallot, and garlic, and sauté for 3 to 5 minutes or until translucent. Add the rice and stir well to coat.

3. Reduce the heat to medium-low, and add the wine to the rice. Stirring frequently, cook for about 5 to 7 minutes or until the rice has absorbed most of the wine. Continuing to stir, add 1 cup of hot stock to the rice, and cook for about 12 minutes or until the rice has absorbed most of the stock.

4. Continue stirring and adding stock 1 cup at a time until all (or most) has been added and the rice is tender but firm. This should take around 45 to 50 minutes.

5. Add the peas, salt, pepper, and any remaining stock to the rice. Stir well, reduce the heat to low, and continue to cook another 5 to 7 minutes or until thick and creamy.

6. Stir the parsley into the risotto and serve.

Yield: 4 to 6 servings

5 cups Vegetable Stock (page 48) or commercial variety

4 tablespoons extra virgin olive oil

$1/2$ cup finely diced onion

I small shallot, finely diced

2 cloves garlic, minced

I cup short-grain brown rice, rinsed and drained

$1/2$ cup dry white wine

2 cups fresh or frozen green peas

I teaspoon sea salt

$1/4$ teaspoon black pepper

$1/4$ cup finely chopped fresh parsley

FOR A CHANGE . . .

- Sauté 1 cup sliced fresh mushrooms with the onions and garlic in Step 2.
- Add small cubes of cooked butternut squash to the rice in Step 4.
- For slightly chewier texture, use $1/2$ cup brown rice and $1/2$ cup pearled barley.
- Add $1/2$ cup diced tomato just before serving.

Mexican Black Beans and Rice

This Mexican-style rice and bean dish is a little spicier than the Spanish-style. If you prefer a milder version, reduce (or omit) the chili powder and/or red pepper flakes.

Yield: 4 to 6 servings

1 tablespoon safflower or extra virgin olive oil

$1/2$ cup diced onion

2 cloves garlic, minced

$1 1/2$ cups short-, medium-, or long-grain brown rice, rinsed and drained

3 cups water

15-ounce can black beans, rinsed and drained

15-ounce can stewed tomatoes (not drained), coarsely chopped

$1/2$ cup diced green bell pepper

2 tablespoons tomato paste

1 teaspoon chili powder, or to taste

$1/2$ teaspoon ground cumin

$1/2$ teaspoon dried oregano

$1/2$ teaspoon sea salt

1 pinch red pepper flakes, or to taste

$1/8$ teaspoon black pepper

1. Heat the oil in a heavy medium-size pot over medium heat. Add the onion and garlic, and sauté for 3 to 4 minutes or until beginning to soften. Add all of the remaining ingredients. Cover and bring to a boil over high heat.

2. Reduce the heat to medium-low, stir once, and cover. Simmer for 45 to 50 minutes or until most of the liquid is absorbed and the rice is tender.

3. Remove from the heat, and let sit for 10 minutes. Transfer the rice and beans to a bowl and serve hot.

FOR A CHANGE . . .

- Substitute pinto or kidney beans for black beans.
- Add $1/2$ cup fresh or frozen sweet corn.
- Substitute hot sauce or salsa for the red pepper flakes.
- For richer flavor, use Vegetable Stock (page 48) instead of water.

A Little Rice Trivia . . .

Nearly 3 million acres of land are used for growing rice in the United States. Arkansas is the leading producer, followed by California, Louisiana, Mississippi, Missouri, and Texas.

Noodles with Parsley-Basil Pesto

Brown rice noodles are tossed with fresh pesto in this flavorful dish, which makes a great entrée, as well as a side. White rice miso adds mild sweetness.

1. Cook the noodles according to package directions.

2. While the noodles are cooking, place all of the remaining ingredients in a blender or food processor, and pulse to form a smooth and creamy pesto.

3. Add the pesto to the cooked noodles, toss, and serve.

FOR A CHANGE . . .

- For a lower-fat pesto, substitute roasted sunflower seeds for the pine nuts.

- Instead of tossing the pesto with the noodles, place the noodles in individual serving bowls, and spoon the desired amount of pesto over each.

Yield: 4 to 5 servings

12 ounces brown rice udon noodles or vermicelli

2 cups chopped, loosely packed fresh basil

2 cups chopped, loosely packed fresh parsley

$1/2$ cup water

$1/4$ cup extra virgin olive oil

$1/2$ cup lightly roasted pine nuts

2 cloves garlic, chopped

2 tablespoons shiro (white rice) miso, or $1/2$ teaspoon sea salt

Spaghetti with Green Pea Pesto

Green peas add a flavorful dimension to the traditional basil pesto in this recipe.

Yield: 4 to 5 servings

12 ounces brown rice spaghetti
or udon noodles

1 ½ cups fresh or frozen green peas

2 cups water for cooking peas

¼ cup extra virgin olive oil

¼ cup lightly roasted pine nuts

1 clove garlic, minced

1 tablespoon shiro (white rice) miso,
or ¼ teaspoon sea salt

1 to 2 tablespoons minced
fresh basil

1 or 2 pinches black pepper

1. Cook the pasta according to package directions.

2. While the pasta is cooking, place the peas and water in a small pot and bring to a boil over high heat. Reduce the heat to medium, and simmer until the peas are tender and bright green (8 to 10 minutes for fresh; 3 to 5 minutes for frozen). Reserving the cooking water, drain the peas and rinse under cold water to set the color. Drain well.

3. Set aside ½ cup of the peas, and place the rest in a blender or food processor along with the oil, pine nuts, garlic, miso, basil, and pepper. Pulse while slowly adding the reserved cooking liquid to form a smooth, creamy, somewhat thick pesto.

4. Add the pesto and reserved peas to the pasta. Toss well, and serve hot, at room temperature, or chilled.

FOR A CHANGE . . .

● For a lower-fat pesto, substitute roasted sunflower seeds for the pine nuts.

Pasta with Sage & Green Peas

A great side dish as well as main course, the pasta in this traditional Italian favorite is served with a luscious sauce of sweet green peas and savory sage.

1. Cook the pasta according to package directions.

2. While the pasta is cooking, heat the oil in a medium skillet over medium-low heat. Add the onions and garlic, and sauté 3 to 5 minutes or until soft and beginning to brown. Add all of the remaining ingredients except the lemon slices, and bring to a boil over high heat.

3. Reduce the heat to medium, and simmer until the peas are tender and bright green (8 to 10 minutes for fresh and 3 to 5 minutes for frozen).

4. Transfer half the peas and cooking liquid to a blender. Pulse for several seconds until smooth, then return to the pot and mix well with the whole peas.

5. Add the pea mixture to the cooked pasta. Toss well, and serve hot.

Yield: 4 to 6 servings

12 ounces any variety brown rice pasta

2 tablespoons extra virgin olive oil

$1/2$ cup finely chopped onions

1 large clove garlic, minced

4 cups fresh or frozen green peas

1 cup Vegetable Stock (page 48) or commercial variety

$1/2$ teaspoon sea salt

$1/4$ teaspoon ground sage

$1/8$ teaspoon black pepper

Fresh lemon slices for garnish

Rice is nice . . . for reviving your cell phone.

If you've dropped your cell phone in water and are able to retrieve it within a few seconds, place it in a bag or bowl of raw rice and leave it there a day or two. If you're lucky, the rice will absorb the moisture and save the phone.

Mediterranean Rice Pilaf

Artichoke hearts, Kalamata olives, and green peas are spotlighted in this light yet flavorful Mediterranean-style pilaf.

Yield: 4 to 6 servings

3 tablespoons extra virgin olive oil

I small onion, diced

I clove garlic, minced

4 cups cooked long-grain brown rice (page 19)*

3 to 4 tablespoons lemon juice

I cup cooked whole wheat or semolina orzo pasta

14-ounce jar water- or brine-packed artichoke hearts, drained and quartered

I cup fresh or frozen green peas

$^1/_2$ cup pitted and halved Kalamata olives

2 tablespoons finely chopped fresh parsley

I tablespoon chopped fresh oregano

$^1/_2$ teaspoon fresh thyme leaves

$^1/_2$ teaspoon sea salt

$^1/_4$ teaspoon black pepper

I cup halved cherry or grape tomatoes for garnish

* Best if the rice is cold or at room temperature. It fries up better than freshly made hot rice.

1. Heat the oil in a large skillet over medium heat. Add the onion and garlic, sauté 1 to 2 minutes, then add the rice and lemon juice. Stir constantly until the rice is hot.

2. Reduce the heat to medium-low, add the orzo, and cook for 3 to 5 minutes, stirring often, or until the mixture is hot.

3. Stir in all of the remaining ingredients except the tomatoes, and cook another 2 to 3 minutes or until the mixture is heated through.

4. Transfer the piping hot pilaf to a serving bowl. Garnish with tomatoes before serving.

FOR A CHANGE . . .

● Add $^1/_4$ cup finely chopped roasted red peppers.

● For added protein and flavor, include $^1/_2$ cup cooked lentils or chickpeas.

Jasmine Spiced Saffron Rice

The aromatic addition of cardamom, cloves, cinnamon, fennel seed, and saffron (the most expensive spice in the world) adds bold flavor and color to this specialty side.

1. Place the cardamom, cloves, cinnamon, and fennel in the center of a 6-inch square piece of cotton cheesecloth. Gather the corners of the cloth together to form a little pouch, and tie securely with cotton string.

2. Place the spice pouch, water, salt, and saffron in a medium pot, and bring to a boil over high heat. Remove from the heat and set aside.

3. Heat the oil in a heavy medium-size pot over medium heat. Add the rice, and stir for 1 to 2 minutes until the grains are coated with oil. Add the raisins and spiced water (including the spice pouch) to the rice. Cover and bring to a boil over high heat.

4. Reduce the heat to medium-low, stir once, and cover. Simmer 40 to 45 minutes or until the liquid is absorbed and the rice is tender. Remove the pot from the heat, discard the spice pouch, and let sit for 10 minutes.

5. While the rice is resting, dry roast the pistachios and almonds in a small skillet for 2 to 3 minutes or until light golden brown. Be careful not to burn.

6. Add the nuts to the rice, fluff with a fork, and transfer to a serving bowl. Enjoy hot.

Yield: 4 to 6 servings

4 cardamom seeds

4 whole cloves

1 cinnamon stick

$1/4$ teaspoon fennel seeds

4 cups water

$1/2$ teaspoon sea salt

1 pinch saffron

2 tablespoons extra virgin olive oil

2 cups brown jasmine rice, rinsed and drained

3 tablespoons raisins

2 tablespoons chopped pistachios

2 tablespoons slivered almonds

FOR A CHANGE . . .

- Add 1 or 2 tablespoons of honey to the spiced cooking liquid for a sweeter flavor.

Spanish-Style Brown Rice

This classic dish is always a winner.
Brown rice and beans provide complete
protein in this version.

Yield: 4 to 6 cups

1 tablespoon extra virgin olive oil

$^1/_2$ cup finely diced onions

2 cloves garlic, minced

$^1/_2$ cup chopped green bell pepper

1$^1/_2$ cups short-, medium-, or long-grain
brown rice, rinsed and drained

3 cups water

15-ounce can pinto beans, rinsed
and drained

15-ounce can stewed tomatoes
(not drained), coarsely chopped

1 cup fresh or frozen sweet corn

3 tablespoons tomato paste

$^1/_2$ teaspoon dried basil

$^1/_2$ teaspoon dried oregano

$^1/_2$ teaspoon ground cumin

$^1/_2$ teaspoon sea salt

$^1/_4$ teaspoon black pepper

3 tablespoons minced fresh parsley

1. Heat the oil in a heavy medium-size pot over medium heat. Add the onion and garlic, and sauté for 2 to 3 minutes or until beginning to soften. Add the green pepper, and continue to sauté for 2 to 3 minutes. Add the rice, and sauté another 3 minutes.

2. Add all remaining ingredients except the parsley. Cover and bring to a boil over high heat. Reduce the heat to medium-low, stir, and cover. Simmer about 1 hour or until the liquid is absorbed and the rice is tender.

3. Remove the pot from the heat, and let sit for 10 minutes. Stir the parsley into the rice, transfer to a serving dish, and enjoy hot.

FOR A CHANGE . . .

- Add 1 or 2 tablespoons minced jalapeño pepper, or a couple dashes of hot sauce for a spicy kick.

- Substitute any variety of bean for the pinto.

- Add $^1/_4$ cup sliced Kalamata olives.

Red Rice Pilaf with Cranberries & Walnuts

*Aromatic red rice has a subtle sweetness that complements
the tangy cranberries and roasted walnuts perfectly
in this delicious pilaf.*

1. Heat the oil in a heavy medium-size pot over medium heat. Add the shallots and garlic, and sauté for 1 to 2 minutes or until beginning to soften.

2. Add the rice, and stir for 1 to 2 minutes until the grains are coated with oil. Add the stock, cranberries, and salt. Cover and bring to a boil over high heat.

3. Reduce the heat to medium-low, stir once, and cover. Simmer 45 to 50 or until the liquid is absorbed and the rice is tender. Remove the pot from the heat and let sit for 10 minutes.

4. Add the walnuts and parsley to the rice, fluff with a fork to mix, and transfer to a serving bowl. Enjoy hot.

FOR A CHANGE . . .

- Try this dish with 1 cup red rice and 1 cup brown basmati.
- Instead of walnuts, use pecans, hazelnuts, pistachios, or slivered almonds
- Although not preferred, you can use water instead of vegetable stock.

Yield: 4 to 6 servings

2 tablespoons extra virgin olive oil

$1/2$ cup finely chopped shallots

1 clove garlic, minced

1 cup red rice, rinsed and drained

1 cup long-grain brown rice, rinsed and drained

4 cups Vegetable Stock (page 48) or commercial variety

$1/2$ cup dried cranberries

1 pinch sea salt

1 cup chopped roasted walnuts

$1/4$ cup minced fresh parsley

Moroccan Rice

Brown rice and chickpeas provide complete protein in this light, mildly sweet Moroccan rice dish, complete with aromatic spices, sweet currants, and richly flavored nuts.

Yield: 4 to 6 servings

2 tablespoons extra virgin olive oil or peanut oil

1 cup finely chopped onion

1 clove garlic, minced

1 cup long-grain brown rice, rinsed and drained

2 cups Vegetable Stock (page 48) or commercial variety

15-ounce can chickpeas, rinsed and drained

$^1/_2$ cup currants or raisins

1$^1/_2$ teaspoons ground turmeric

$^1/_4$ teaspoon ground cinnamon

$^1/_4$ teaspoon ground ginger

$^1/_2$ cup roasted slivered almonds

$^1/_4$ cup minced fresh mint or parsley

Lemon wedges for garnish

1. Heat the oil in a heavy medium-size pot over medium-low heat. Add the onion and garlic, and sauté for 2 to 3 minutes or until beginning to soften. Add the rice and sauté another 2 minutes.

2. Add the stock, chickpeas, currants, turmeric, cinnamon, and ginger to the pot. Cover and bring to a boil over high heat.

3. Reduce the heat to medium-low, stir once, and cover. Simmer for 45 to 50 minutes or until the liquid is absorbed and the rice is tender. Remove from the heat and let sit for 10 minutes.

4. Add the almonds and mint to the rice, fluff with a fork to mix, and transfer to a serving bowl. Serve with lemon wedges for added flavor.

FOR A CHANGE . . .

• Substitute brown basmati for the long-grain brown rice.

A WORD ABOUT WILD RICE

When it comes to wild rice, it's important to be aware that much of what is sold today is actually cultivated paddy-grown rice that has been harvested and processed by machine—not true wild rice. I prefer authentic Native American hand-harvested wild rice, which is available in most natural foods stores. Compared to dark paddy-grown varieties, it has a lighter color and fluffier texture. It is also nuttier in flavor, which it gets from traditional wood-fire parching. I recommend it for the recipes in this book, although paddy-grown wild rice also works.

Native American Wild Rice

Wild rice is the only traditional grain of North America. It was a staple of Native Americans, especially those who lived in the northern woodlands, where it grew abundantly in lakes. Nuts, wild mushrooms, and berries were other popular Native American foods. This dish, which combines all of these traditional ingredients with brown rice, is one of my favorites. For the best flavor and texture, be sure to look for authentic hand-harvested wild rice.

1. Heat the oil in a heavy medium-size pot over medium heat. Add the onion and garlic, and sauté for 2 to 3 minutes or until beginning to soften. Add the mushrooms, and sauté another 2 to 3 minutes or until they release their juice.

2. Add all of the remaining ingredients to the pot except the pine nuts and parsley. Cover and bring to a boil over high heat.

3. Reduce the heat to medium-low, stir once, and cover. Simmer for 30 to 35 minutes or until the liquid is absorbed and the rice is tender and fluffy. Remove from the heat and let sit 10 minutes.

4. Remove and discard the bay leaf. Add the pine nuts and parsley to the rice, fluff with a fork to mix, and transfer to a serving bowl. Enjoy hot.

FOR A CHANGE . . .

- Instead of Vegetable Stock, use Mushroom Stock (page 49).
- Substitute chopped pecans, walnuts, or hazelnuts for the pine nuts.
- Use thyme instead of sage.

Yield: 4 to 6 servings

1 tablespoon extra virgin olive or safflower oil

1 small onion, finely diced

1 clove garlic, minced

$1/2$ cup chopped fresh mushrooms, any variety

1 cup wild rice, rinsed and drained*

1 cup long-grain brown rice, rinsed and drained

$4^1/2$ cups Vegetable Stock (page 48) or commercial variety

$1/3$ cup dried cranberries, wild blueberries, or raisins

$1/4$ cup finely diced celery

$1/4$ cup finely diced carrot

$1/2$ teaspoon ground sage

$1/4$ teaspoon sea salt

1 bay leaf

$1/4$ cup lightly roasted pine nuts

2 tablespoons minced parsley

* Native American hand-harvested wild rice is preferred (see page 130).

Curried Rice with Dried Apricots

I strongly recommend using Turkish apricots for this dish. They are much sweeter, softer, and more flavorful than traditional dried apricots. (Furthermore, traditional varieties are often sulfured, and they must be soaked at least thirty minutes before using.) Turkish apricots are readily available at most natural foods stores and Middle Eastern markets.

Yield: 4 to 6 servings

2 cups long-grain brown rice or brown basmati rice, rinsed and drained

3 $^1/_2$ cups water

1 cup coarsely chopped Turkish apricots

$^1/_2$ cup fresh orange juice

2 teaspoons curry powder

$^1/_4$ teaspoon ground cinnamon

1 pinch cayenne pepper

1 pinch sea salt

Roasted pistachios for garnish

Minced parsley for garnish

1. Place all of ingredients except the pistachios and parsley in a heavy medium-size pot. Cover and bring to a boil over high heat.

2. Reduce the heat to medium-low, stir once, and cover. Simmer for 45 to 50 minutes or until the liquid is absorbed and the rice is tender. Remove from the heat and let sit for 10 minutes.

3. Garnish with pistachios and parsley. Serve hot.

FOR A CHANGE . . .

● Before adding the ingredients to the pot in Step 1, sauté $^1/_2$ cup diced onions in 1 tablespoon olive oil.

● Instead of the apricots, use dried cranberries, raisins, or currants.

● For a richer flavor, use Vegetable Stock (page 48) instead of water.

● Use pineapple juice instead of orange juice.

A Little Rice Trivia . . .

In the United States, National Rice Month is celebrated in September.

Baked Herbed Rice and Lentils

Dried fruit adds a spark of sweetness to this savory nutty-flavored rice dish, which offers complete protein thanks to the lentils!

1. Preheat the oven to 350°F.

2. Place the rice in heavy medium-sized skillet over medium heat. Stirring often, dry roast the rice for 5 to 7 minutes or until it releases a nutty aroma and turns slightly golden in color.

3. Transfer the roasted rice to a 13-x-9-inch baking dish. Add all remaining ingredients except the parsley and mix well. Cover the dish with foil or a tight-fitting lid. Bake for 1 hour or until the liquid is absorbed and the rice and lentils are tender.

4. Remove from the oven and let sit for 10 minutes. Discard the bay leaves, add the parsley to the rice, and gently mix before serving.

FOR A CHANGE . . .

- For richer flavor, use Vegetable Stock (page 48) or Mushroom Stock (page 49) instead of water.

Yield: 4 to 6 servings

1 cup long-grain brown rice or brown basmati rice, rinsed and drained

1 cup lentils, rinsed and drained

4 cups boiling water

$^1/_2$ cup currants, raisins, and/or dried cranberries

$^1/_2$ teaspoon ground cumin

$^1/_4$ teaspoon ground thyme

2 bay leaves

$^1/_4$ teaspoon sea salt

$^1/_8$ teaspoon black pepper

$^1/_4$ cup minced fresh parsley

Mujaddarah
Spiced Rice & Lentils

*This Middle Eastern classic is tasty, refreshing, and very
simple to make. It's usually made with long-grain white rice,
but I prefer more nutritious long-grain brown rice or even
aromatic brown basmati rice. Mujaddarah is traditionally
served with flatbread and plain yogurt or sour cream.
I recommend soy yogurt or tofu sour cream.*

Yield: 4 to 6 servings

1 cup long-grain brown rice
or brown basmati rice,
rinsed and drained

4 cups water, divided

1 cup brown lentils,
rinsed and drained

3 tablespoons extra virgin
olive oil, divided

4 cups sliced onions

1 cup finely chopped fresh parsley

3/4 teaspoon ground cumin

1 teaspoon sea salt

1/4 teaspoon ground cinnamon

1/4 teaspoon black pepper

1. Place the rice and 1³/₄ cups of the water in a heavy
medium-size pot. Cover and bring to a boil over high heat.
Reduce the heat to medium-low, stir once, and cover. Simmer for 45 to 50 minutes or until the water is absorbed and
the rice is tender.

2. In another medium-size pot, add the lentils and the
remaining 2¹/₄ cups water. Cover and bring to a boil over
high heat. Reduce the heat to medium-low, and simmer
for 40 to 45 minutes or until the lentils are tender.

3. While the rice and lentils are cooking, heat 1¹/₂ tablespoons of the oil in a large skillet over medium-high heat.
Add the onions and sauté, stirring constantly, for about
5 minutes. Reduce the heat to low, cover, and simmer for
20 to 25 minutes or until caramelized and golden brown.
Set aside.

4. When the rice is done, remove from the heat, and let sit
for 10 minutes. When the lentils are done, remove from
the heat, and let cool. Drain and discard any remaining
cooking liquid.

5. Transfer the rice and lentils to a mixing bowl. Add the
remaining oil, the parsley, cumin, salt, cinnamon, and black
pepper. Mix well.

6. Place the mujaddarah in a serving bowl. Top with cara-melized onions and serve as is or with a dollop of soy yogurt or Tofu Sour Cream (page 74).

FOR A CHANGE . . .

- For added spice and a bit of heat, add 1 clove minced garlic and 1 small minced chili pepper to the dish.

- For a slightly easier version, use a 15-ounce can of lentils (drained) instead of dried.

Lemon Cardamom Basmati Rice

Zesty lemon and fragrant cardamom add wonderful flavor to aromatic basmati rice in this easy-to-prepare Middle Eastern favorite.

1. Place the rice, water, cardamom, and lemon grass in a heavy medium-size pot. Cover and bring to a boil over high heat.

2. Reduce the heat to medium-low, stir once, and cover. Simmer 45 to 50 minutes or until the liquid is absorbed and the rice is tender.

3. Remove the pot from the heat, and let sit for 10 min-utes. Remove and discard the cardamom and lemon grass.

4. Transfer the rice to a serving bowl. Garnish with almonds and parsley, and serve.

Yield: 4 to 6 servings

2 cups brown basmati rice, rinsed and drained

4 cups cold water

6 cardamom seeds

6- to 8-inch piece lemon grass, cut into 1- to 2-inch pieces

1 pinch sea salt

Roasted slivered almonds for garnish

Minced parsley or mint for garnish

Fried Rice with Peppers and Edamame

*Bell peppers and edamame add a pop of color
to this Asian-inspired fried rice dish.*

Yield: 4 to 6 servings

2 tablespoons sesame or
extra virgin olive oil

2 cloves garlic, minced

$1/2$ cup diced red bell pepper

$1/2$ cup diced yellow bell pepper

4 cups cooked short-, medium-,
or long-grain brown rice
(page 19)

1 cup shelled edamame

$1 1/2$ tablespoons shoyu soy sauce,
or to taste

$1/3$ cup chopped scallions

1. Heat the oil in large skillet or wok over medium-high heat. Add the garlic and peppers, and stir-fry 2 to 3 minutes or until the peppers begin to soften.

2. Add the rice, edamame, and shoyu, and continue to stir-fry for 3 to 5 minutes or until the rice is hot and the edamame are tender and bright green.

3. Stir in the scallions, and continue to cook another 2 to 3 minutes. Serve hot.

FOR A CHANGE . . .

● For a spark of heat, add $1/4$ to $1/2$ teaspoon hot pepper sesame oil in Step 1.

● Sauté $1/2$ cup sliced fresh mushrooms with the garlic and peppers in Step 1.

8

The Main Event

Looking for some delectable brown rice entrées? Well, you've come to the right place. In this chapter, a parade of national and international culinary delights awaits, so get ready to take a trip around the country and throughout the world.

Among the all-American main-dish favorites on the following pages, you'll find recipes for Savory Stuffed Cabbage, hearty Rice & Bean Burgers, heavenly Stuffed Baked Squash, and a simple but sensational Baked Rice and Barley Casserole. Representing the South, there is a classic recipe for Louisiana Red Beans and Rice, as well as a vegetarian version of Louisiana Dirty Rice that's "dirtied" with seitan. You'll also find another Southern favorite, black-eyed peas, which are served piping hot over a bed of brown rice.

There is Spanish-style Vegetarian Tempeh Paella, Italian-inspired Spaghetti with Mushroom Marinara, and Indonesian Peanut Pasta made with brown rice vermicelli. The Rice 'n Bean Enchiladas and the Brown Rice and Bean Burritos from Mexico are spicy and filling, as are the Pad Thai noodles from Thailand. Falafel Pockets represent the Middle East, while Chinese classics include Vegetable Chow Mein, Lo Mein, and Chop Suey. And if Indian food is your passion, be sure to try the creamy Red Lentil Dal and the Curried Chickpeas & Brown Rice.

Some of these dishes are complete meals in themselves, while others need only a fresh salad or vegetable side as the perfect accompaniment. But no matter which dish you choose, all are delightfully delicious and sure to please.

Savory Stuffed Cabbage

Brown rice, buckwheat, and lentils are the perfect combination for vegan stuffed cabbage, while the rich, savory tomato sauce complements and balances. Be sure to make extra, because stuffed cabbage always tastes better the next day, when all flavors have blended.

Yield: 12 to 14 rolls

1 medium head green cabbage

About 2 quarts (8 cups) water
for cooking cabbage

FILLING

2 tablespoons extra virgin olive oil

$^1/_2$ cup diced onion

2 cloves garlic, minced

$^1/_2$ cup long-grain brown rice,
rinsed and drained

$^1/_2$ cup buckwheat groats or
toasted buckwheat (kasha),
rinsed and drained

2 cups cold water

$^1/_4$ teaspoon sea salt

$^1/_8$ teaspoon black pepper

1 cup cooked lentils (rinse if canned)

SAUCE

3 cups water

2 cups tomato sauce

4 teaspoons apple cider vinegar

2 teaspoons ground cumin

1 teaspoon sea salt

$^1/_2$ teaspoon black pepper

1. Remove and discard any damaged leaves from the cabbage, and cut out the core with a paring knife. Set aside.

2. To prepare the filling, heat the oil in heavy medium-size pot over medium heat. Add the onion and garlic, and sauté for 4 to 5 minutes or until beginning to soften.

3. Add all of the remaining filling ingredients except the lentils to the pot. Cover and bring to a boil over high heat. Reduce the heat to medium-low, stir, and cover. Simmer 45 to 50 minutes or until the water is absorbed and the grains are tender. Remove from the heat, add the lentils, and mix well. Set aside to cool.

4. While the grains are cooking, bring about 2 quarts of water to a boil in a large pot. Place the entire cabbage core-side down in the boiling water, cover, and cook for 5 to 7 minutes. Remove the cabbage, and peel off the outer leaves that are tender and loosen easily. Set the leaves aside and

**Preparing
Cabbage Rolls**

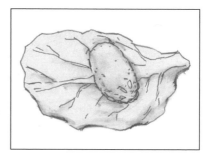

1. Spoon the filling in the center
of the leaf.

return the cabbage to the boiling water. Repeat until you have 12 to 14 leaves.

5. Place about 3 to 4 tablespoons of the filling mixture in the center of each cabbage leaf (see Step 1 on page 138). Fold the sides of the leaf toward the center over the filling. Then roll up from the bottom to form the packet (see Step 2). Place the rolls seam side down on a plate and set aside.

6. Preheat the oven to 350°F. Combine all of the sauce ingredients and set aside.

7. Line the bottom of a 13-x-9-inch baking dish with 3 or 4 whole cabbage leaves, and place the stuffed cabbage rolls on top (see Step 3). The leaves will help prevent the rolls from burning. Pour the sauce over the rolls.

8. Cover the baking dish with foil. Bake for 45 to 60 minutes or until the rolls are very tender. Cool slightly before serving.

FOR A CHANGE . . .

- Replace the buckwheat with millet or wild rice.
- Use cooked chickpeas instead of lentils.
- Instead of green cabbage, use quickly blanched collard, chard, or Chinese cabbage leaves, and reduce the baking time by half. Be careful not to overblanch the leaves, which are more delicate than cabbage leaves.
- Rather than baking the rolls in the oven, simmer them in covered pot on the stove over very low heat for $1\frac{1}{2}$ to 2 hours.

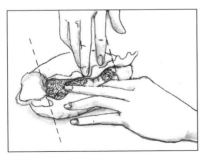

2. Fold the right and left sides over the filling, then roll up from the bottom to form a packet.

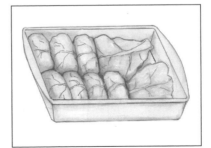

3. Place the filled rolls seam side down in the baking dish.

Yield: 3 to 4 servings

8 ounces brown rice udon noodles

1 tablespoon extra virgin olive oil

1 tablespoon toasted sesame oil

1 teaspoon hot pepper sesame oil or chili oil

1 cup chopped red onion

2 cloves garlic, minced

1 cup sliced fresh shiitake mushroom caps

$\frac{1}{2}$ cup julienned carrots

$\frac{1}{4}$ cup thinly sliced celery

1 cup fresh bean sprouts

1 cup chopped Chinese cabbage or bok choy

$\frac{1}{2}$ cup sliced red bell pepper

$\frac{1}{2}$ cup snow peas or snap peas, stems removed

SAUCE

3 tablespoons kuzu root starch

1 cup water

$1\frac{1}{2}$ tablespoons shoyu soy sauce, or $\frac{1}{2}$ teaspoon sea salt

$1\frac{1}{2}$ tablespoons maple syrup or honey

1 teaspoon brown rice vinegar

2 teaspoons finely grated fresh ginger

Vegetable Lo Mein

Brown rice udon noodles are tossed with fresh vegetables and a flavorful sauce in this popular Chinese dish.

1. Cook the noodles according to package directions. Rinse, drain, and set aside.

2. Heat the oils in a wok or large skillet over medium heat. Add the onion and garlic, and sauté for 2 to 3 minutes or until beginning to soften. Add the shiitake, and sauté another 2 to 3 minutes or until soft.

3. Place all of the sauce ingredients in a small bowl. Mix with a fork or whisk until the kuzu is dissolved. Add to the wok while stirring constantly. Add the carrots and celery, and continue to stir for 2 to 3 minutes or until the sauce thickens.

4. Add the cabbage, bell pepper, snow peas, and noodles. Mix well and continue to cook 2 to 3 minutes or until the snow peas and cabbage are tender yet crisp, and the noodles are hot.

5. Transfer to a serving platter and enjoy!

A Little Rice Trivia . . .

China is the largest producer of the world's rice—nearly 30 percent—followed by India, which produces about 22 percent.

Chop Suey

Served over a bed of brown rice, this quick and easy-to-prepare Chinese classic contains mushrooms and an assortment of fresh vegetables in a rich sauce.

1. Heat the oils in a 4-quart pot over medium heat. Add the onion and shiitake, and sauté for 2 to 3 minutes or until beginning to soften. Add the carrots, celery, and peppers, and sauté another 2 to 3 minutes.

2. Dissolve the kuzu in the cold water and set aside.

3. Add the stock, broccoli, and tofu to the pot. Increase the heat and bring the ingredients to a boil. Reduce the heat to medium-low, add the water chestnuts, shoyu, and the dissolved kuzu. Simmer while stirring constantly for 3 to 5 minutes or until the sauce thickens.

4. Reduce the heat to low, add the scallions, bean sprouts, snow peas, and ginger. Stir and continue to simmer for another 2 to 3 minutes or until the snow peas are bright green yet crisp.

5. Spoon the piping hot chop suey over individual servings of brown rice. Serve immediately.

FOR A CHANGE . . .

- Substitute deep-fried tofu cubes for the fresh.
- For a spicier kick, increase the hot pepper oil or add a dash of hot sauce.
- Although not preferred, you can use water instead of vegetable stock.
- Try including other fresh vegetables. Yellow summer squash, zucchini, cauliflower florets, green bell pepper, and Chinese cabbage are all good choices.
- In place of tofu, add freshly steamed shrimp, cubed seitan, or deep-fried tempeh during the last few minutes of cooking.
- Serve over Crispy Rice Noodles (page 85) or any brown rice pasta.

Yield: 4 to 6 servings

2 teaspoons toasted sesame oil

$^1/_2$ teaspoon hot pepper sesame oil

I cup onion wedges

$^1/_2$ cup quartered fresh shiitake mushroom caps

$^1/_2$ cup julienned carrots

$^1/_4$ cup sliced celery

$^1/_3$ cup chopped red, yellow, or orange bell pepper

$^1/_3$ cup kuzu root starch

$^1/_3$ cup cold water

4 cups Vegetable Stock (page 48) or commercial variety

I cup small broccoli florets

I cup tofu cubes

$^1/_3$ cup sliced water chestnuts

I $^1/_2$ tablespoons shoyu soy sauce, or to taste

$^1/_3$ cup cut scallions (I $^1/_2$-inch pieces)

$^1/_4$ cup fresh bean sprouts

$^1/_2$ cup snow peas, stems removed

2 teaspoons finely grated fresh ginger

4 cups freshly cooked short-, medium-, or long-grain brown rice (page 19)

Red Lentil Dal

Dal, a staple Indian dish, is made with any variety of lentils or split peas, cooked with aromatic spices, and served over rice. This flavorful version is made with red lentils. It's creamy and comforting.

Yield: 4 to 6 servings

2 cups brown basmati or long-grain brown rice, rinsed and drained

4 cups water

1 pinch sea salt

DAL

$1/4$ cup safflower or extra virgin olive oil

1 large red, Spanish, or Vidalia onion, coarsely chopped

3 cloves garlic, minced

2 cups red lentils, rinsed and drained

6 to 7 cups cold water

1 jalapeño or serrano chile pepper, seeded and minced

$1 1/2$ tablespoons finely chopped fresh ginger

1 tablespoon curry powder

$1/2$ teaspoon ground cinnamon

$1/2$ teaspoon ground turmeric

$1/2$ teaspoon ground cumin

$1/4$ teaspoon yellow mustard seeds

1 teaspoon sea salt

$1/4$ teaspoon black pepper

2 cups cut green beans (2-inch pieces), blanched

3 tablespoons fresh lemon juice

$1/4$ cup minced fresh parsley

1. Place the rice, water, and salt in a heavy medium-size pot. Cover and bring to a boil over high heat. Reduce the heat to medium-low, stir once, and cover. Simmer for 45 to 50 minutes or until the water is absorbed and the rice is tender.

2. While the rice is cooking, heat the oil in another medium pot over medium heat. Add the onions and garlic, and sauté 4 to 5 minutes or until beginning to soften.

3. Add the lentils, half the water, the jalapeño, ginger, curry powder, cinnamon, turmeric, cumin, and mustard seeds. Increase the heat and bring to a boil.

4. Reduce the heat to medium-low, and cover the pot with the lid slightly ajar. Stirring occasionally, simmer for 15 to 20 minutes. Add the remaining water, and continue to simmer another 20 minutes or until the lentils are cooked. (The mixture should not be too thick or too runny. Add more water if necessary.)

5. Reduce the heat to low, add the salt, pepper, green beans, and lemon juice. Continue to cook 5 to 7 minutes or until the green beans are tender and the dal is soft and creamy. Add the parsley.

6. Ladle the piping hot dal over individual servings of brown rice.

FOR A CHANGE . . .

● Experiment with other flavorful spices. Ground coriander and fennel seeds are good choices.

- Substitute lime juice for the lemon juice.
- Instead of green beans, use asparagus.
- For richer flavor, use Vegetable Stock (page 48) instead of water to cook the rice and lentils.
- Add a little water to leftover dal, mix in some cooked rice, and enjoy as soup the next day.

Baked Rice and Barley Casserole

Baked rice casseroles are especially nice during cooler seasons when you don't mind using the oven. This one is nourishing, comforting, and surprisingly light and fluffy. Barley adds a delightfully chewy texture.

1. Preheat the oven to 350°F.

2. Place the brown rice and barley in a heavy medium-sized skillet over medium-low heat. Stirring occasionally, dry roast the grains for 5 to 7 minutes or until they release a nutty aroma and turn slightly golden. Transfer to a 13-x-9-inch baking dish and set aside.

3. Place the mushrooms and stock in a medium pot over high heat. Cover and bring to a boil. Reduce the heat to medium-low, and simmer about 5 minutes or until the mushrooms are soft.

4. Add the mushrooms and stock to the baking dish along with the chickpeas, cranberries, sage, salt, and pepper. Mix well and cover. Bake for 1 hour or until the liquid is absorbed and the rice is tender.

5. Stir the pecans and parsley into the cooked rice. Serve piping hot.

Yield: 4 to 6 servings

1 cup long-grain brown rice, rinsed and drained

1 cup partially pearled barley, rinsed and drained

$1/3$ cup any variety dried mushrooms

6 cups Vegetable Stock (page 48) or commercial variety

2 cups cooked chickpeas (rinse if canned)

$1/4$ cup dried cranberries

$1/4$ teaspoon ground sage or poultry seasoning

$1/4$ teaspoon sea salt

$1/8$ teaspoon black pepper

$1/3$ cup lightly roasted pecan pieces

2 tablespoons minced fresh parsley

Curried Vegetables over Rice

Whether it is served over brown rice, white rice, or pasta, the curried vegetable sauce in this recipe is always a hit. Rich, creamy, comforting . . .

Yield: 4 to 6 servings

4 to 6 cups cooked short-, medium-, or long-grain brown rice (page 19)

Roasted cashews for garnish

Finely minced parsley or chives for garnish

VEGETABLE SAUCE

3 tablespoons extra virgin olive, safflower, or peanut oil

1 cup diced onion or shallots

3 cloves garlic, minced

$\frac{1}{2}$ cup diced white button mushrooms

2 cups Vegetable Stock (page 48) or commercial variety

2 small potatoes, diced

1 cup cubed butternut squash

$\frac{1}{2}$ cup cooked chickpeas (rinse if canned)

$\frac{1}{4}$ cup diced celery

$\frac{3}{4}$ teaspoon sea salt

2 cups plain unsweetened soymilk

3 tablespoons unbleached white or pastry flour

2 teaspoons curry powder

$\frac{1}{2}$ teaspoon ground turmeric

$\frac{1}{4}$ teaspoon ground cumin

$\frac{1}{4}$ teaspoon ground cinnamon

1 pinch cayenne pepper

$\frac{1}{2}$ cup blanched fresh or frozen green peas

1. To prepare the sauce, heat the oil in a medium pot over medium heat. Add the onion and garlic, and sauté for 4 to 5 minutes or until slightly golden. Add the mushrooms, sauté another 2 to 3 minutes, then add the stock, potatoes, squash, chickpeas, celery, and salt.

2. Bring the ingredients to a boil over high heat. Reduce the heat to medium-low, stir, and cover. Simmer for 7 to 10 minutes or until the potatoes and squash are tender.

3. Whisk together the soymilk and flour until smooth. Slowly add the mixture to the pot, stirring constantly for 4 to 5 minutes or until the sauce begins to thicken. Do not boil or the soymilk will curdle.

4. Reduce the heat to low, add all of the remaining sauce ingredients, and simmer 2 to 3 minutes.

5. Ladle the curried vegetables over individual servings of brown rice. Garnish with cashews and parsley before serving.

FOR A CHANGE . . .

- Use any variety of fresh mushrooms.
- Try a variety of other vegetables, such as carrots, cauliflower, broccoli, and zucchini.
- Substitute buttercup, sweet dumpling, or delicata squash for the butternut.
- Although not preferred, you can use water instead of vegetable stock.

Vegetarian Tempeh Paella

A traditional Spanish dish, paella is made with white rice, vegetables, and often seafood or some type of meat. Its essential seasoning is saffron, the world's most expensive spice. This vegetarian version is made with nutritious whole grain brown rice. The addition of tempeh provides complete nutrition.

1. Place the brown rice in a medium skillet over medium-low heat. Stirring occasionally, dry roast the rice for 5 to 7 minutes or until it releases a nutty aroma and turns slightly golden. Remove from the heat and set aside.

2. Heat the oil in a heavy medium-size pot over medium-low heat. Add the shallots and garlic, and sauté for 4 to 5 minutes or until beginning to soften. Add the rice, stock, tomato paste, paprika, saffron, salt, and pepper. Increase the heat to high, cover, and bring to a boil.

3. Reduce the heat to medium-low, cover, and simmer the ingredients for 35 to 40 minutes. Add all of the remaining ingredients, gently stir, and cover. Continue to simmer another 10 to 15 minutes or until most of the liquid is absorbed, and the rice and vegetables are tender.

4. Serve the paella as is or with a garnish of minced parsley, chives, or scallions.

FOR A CHANGE . . .

- For a different flavor, add $1/8$ teaspoon curry powder and $1/8$ teaspoon ground cinnamon to the rice as it simmers.
- For seafood paella, omit the tempeh and add 1 cup medium shrimp, 6 to 8 small clams, and 6 to 8 mussels (all left in their shells, which should be scrubbed clean). Place on top of the rice (do not mix) during the last 5 to 7 minutes of cooking and let steam. Serve with fresh lemon wedges.
- Although not preferred, you can use water instead of vegetable stock.

Yield: 4 to 6 servings

$1 1/2$ cups long-grain brown rice, rinsed and drained

3 tablespoons extra virgin olive oil

$1/2$ cup finely chopped shallots

3 cloves garlic, minced

3 cups Vegetable Stock (page 48) or commercial variety

1 tablespoon tomato paste

1 teaspoon sweet or smoked paprika

$1/2$ teaspoon crushed saffron threads

$1/2$ teaspoon sea salt

$1/8$ teaspoon black pepper

1 cup deep-fried or pan-fried tempeh cubes

2 medium tomatoes, chopped

1 small red bell pepper, diced

$1/4$ cup fresh or frozen sweet corn

$1/4$ cup coarsely chopped fresh green beans

Louisiana Dirty Rice with Seitan

Sometimes called Cajun rice, this Southern classic got its name because it was "dirtied" with browned chicken livers and giblets. This healthier low-fat vegetarian version is "dirtied" with seitan.

Yield: 4 to 6 servings

2 cups brown basmati rice, rinsed and drained

4 cups Vegetable Stock (page 48) or commercial variety

1 pinch sea salt

3 tablespoons extra virgin olive oil, divided

1 pound finely chopped or coarsely ground seitan

$^1/_2$ cup diced onion

$^1/_2$ cup diced celery

$^1/_2$ cup diced green bell pepper

1 jalapeño pepper, seeded and minced

2 teaspoons Cajun seasoning

$^1/_2$ cup chopped scallions

Chopped fresh parsley for garnish

1. Place the rice, stock, and salt in a heavy medium-size pot. Cover and bring to a boil over high heat. Reduce the heat to low, stir once, and cover. Simmer 45 to 50 minutes or until the liquid is absorbed and the rice is tender. Remove from the heat and let sit 5 minutes.

2. Spread out the rice on a baking sheet, drizzle with 1 tablespoon of the olive oil, and gently mix. Set aside and let cool.

3. While the rice is cooling, heat the remaining oil in a large skillet over medium-low heat. Add the seitan, and cook for 2 to 3 minutes or until slightly browned.

4. Add the onion, celery, bell pepper, and jalapeño pepper to the skillet. Stir frequently until bits of seitan and vegetables begin to stick to the bottom of the skillet and start to get brown and crispy. If necessary, lower the heat to prevent burning.

5. Add about $^1/_2$ cup water to the skillet. Scrape the bottom with a spatula to loosen the bits of seitan and vegetables. Add the Cajun seasoning, increase the heat to high, and stir frequently until most of the liquid has evaporated. Add the rice and mix to combine.

6. Remove from the heat and stir in the scallions. Garnish with parsley and serve.

FOR A CHANGE . . .

- For a spicier flavor, add a few drops of hot sauce in Step 5.
- Substitute any variety of tempeh (ground or finely chopped) for the seitan.
- Use any color or combination of bell peppers.

Falafel Pockets

The quickest way to prepare this classic Middle Eastern chickpea treat is with falafel mix, which is available in most natural foods markets and grocery stores. In this recipe, brown rice and cooked chickpeas are added to the mix for increased texture and nutrition.

1. Prepare the falafel according to package directions. Add the brown rice and chickpeas to the mixture, and stir until well combined. Let sit 20 minutes or until the mixture is firm enough to hold together.

2. Form the mixture into 2-inch balls (about 14 to 16). Flatten the balls slightly into patties, and set aside.

3. Heat 2 to 3-inches of oil in a deep fryer or medium pot over medium-high heat. Carefully add a few falafel at a time to the hot oil (do not crowd the pot), and deep-fry for 3 to 5 minutes or until golden brown. Remove and place on paper towels to absorb any oil.

4. Heat the pita rounds in the oven or toaster oven. Remove and cut in half.

5. Tuck 2 falafel into each pita half along with tomatoes, cucumbers, and lettuce. Drizzle with sauce and enjoy!

Yield: 7 or 8 pockets

4 whole wheat pita rounds

2 medium tomatoes, sliced or chopped

I large cucumber, sliced

Several romaine lettuce leaves, chopped

Tahini-Lemon Sauce (page 68)

FALAFEL

6-ounce box falafel mix

I cup cooked short-, medium-, or long-grain brown rice (page 19)

$1/2$ cup mashed chickpeas

Safflower oil for frying

Curried Chickpeas & Brown Rice

*Curry sauce is always a big hit when served over brown rice.
In this dish, the rice is part of the dish itself.*

Yield: 4 to 6 servings

2 tablespoons extra virgin olive oil

$^1/_2$ cup minced shallots or onion

2 cloves garlic, minced

2 cups brown basmati or long-grain
brown rice, rinsed and drained

4 cups cold water

I cup cooked chickpeas
(rinse if canned)

$^1/_2$ cup raisins

$^1/_4$ cup diced carrots

$^1/_4$ cup diced celery

I $^1/_2$ teaspoons curry powder

$^1/_4$ teaspoon ground cinnamon

$^1/_8$ teaspoon cayenne pepper

I pinch sea salt

$^1/_4$ cup blanched fresh or frozen
green peas

Chopped roasted cashews
for garnish

1. Heat the oil in a heavy medium-size pot over medium-low heat. Add the shallots and garlic, and sauté for 2 to 3 minutes or until beginning to soften. Stir in the rice, and continue to sauté another 2 to 3 minutes.

2. Add all of the remaining ingredients except the green peas and cashews to the pot. Cover and bring to a boil over high heat. Reduce the heat to low, stir, and cover. Simmer for 45 to 50 minutes or until most of the liquid is absorbed and the rice is tender.

3. Remove the pot from the heat, and let sit for 10 minutes. Add the peas and transfer to a serving bowl. Garnish with cashews and serve.

FOR A CHANGE . . .

- For richer flavor, use Vegetable Stock (page 48) instead of water.

A Little Rice Trivia . . .

The United States produces less than 2 percent of the world's rice, but ranks fourth as its exporter. Nearly half of the country's annual crop is sent primarily to Mexico, Central America, and the Caribbean.

Stuffed Baked Squash

You'll find the stuffing in this recipe light and fluffy. Wild rice, pecans, and cranberries offer a delectable variety of flavors and textures.

1. Preheat the oven to 350°F. Cut each squash in half and remove the seeds. Lightly coat the outside of each half with safflower oil and place on a baking sheet. Set aside.

2. To prepare the stuffing, heat the oil in a medium skillet over medium heat. Add the shallots, and sauté for 2 to 3 minutes or until beginning to brown. Add the celery, mushrooms, and salt, and sauté another 4 to 5 minutes or until the mushrooms release their juice.

3. Transfer the sautéed vegetables to a medium mixing bowl along with the remaining stuffing ingredients. Mix until well combined.

4. Fill the squash halves with stuffing, cover each with foil, and bake 45 to 50 minutes or until the squash is tender when poked with a fork. Remove the foil and bake another 7 to 10 minutes to brown slightly.

5. Garnish with chives before serving

FOR A CHANGE . . .

- Substitute roasted walnuts or hazelnuts for the pecans.
- Instead of cranberries, try dried blueberries or coarsely chopped dried cherries.

Yield: 4 servings

2 medium acorn squash

Safflower oil for coating squash

Minced chives, parsley or scallions for garnish

STUFFING

2 tablespoons safflower oil

$1/4$ cup finely chopped shallots or onions

$1/4$ cup finely diced celery

I cup finely diced fresh crimini or button mushrooms

$1/8$ teaspoon sea salt

I cup cooked long-grain brown rice (page 19)

I cup cooked wild rice*

$1/2$ cup coarsely chopped roasted pecans

$1/2$ cup dried cranberries

$1/2$ teaspoon poultry seasoning

$1/4$ teaspoon ground thyme

* Native American hand-harvested wild rice is preferred (see page 130).

Louisiana Red Beans and Rice

Red beans and rice is a Louisiana specialty. Traditionally, Monday in the "Big Easy" was considered laundry day, so making a dish that didn't require a lot of attention—one that could be left to slowly simmer while doing the wash—was important. Today, you can still find several restaurants serving this hearty bean-and-rice classic on any given Monday. Although this dish is typically made with meat, this vegan variation with seitan is healthier, yet still offers the wonderfully complex flavors of the classic version.

Yield: 4 to 6 servings

1 pound dry kidney beans, sorted and rinsed

2 teaspoons extra virgin olive or safflower oil

3 cups chopped Vidalia or Spanish onions

3 cloves garlic, minced

1 large red bell pepper, chopped

1 1/2 cups cubed seitan

2 stalks celery, chopped

3 bay leaves

1 teaspoon smoked paprika

1/2 teaspoon dried thyme

1/2 teaspoon sea salt

1/2 teaspoon dried oregano

1/4 teaspoon cayenne pepper

1/4 teaspoon black pepper

4 to 6 cups cooked long-grain brown rice or brown basmati rice (page 19)

1. Place the beans in a large bowl, cover with around 2- to 3-inches cold water, and let soak 6 to 8 hours or overnight. Discard the soaking water, rinse the soaked beans, and drain.

2. Heat the oil in a Dutch oven or heavy 4-quart pot over medium heat. Add the onion and garlic, and sauté for 3 to 5 minutes or until beginning to soften. Add the bell pepper and sauté another 2 to 3 minutes while stirring frequently.

3. Add all of the remaining ingredients except the cooked rice to the pot. Add enough water to cover the beans by 2 inches. Cover and bring to a boil over high heat.

4. Reduce the heat to medium-low, and simmer for about 1 1/2 hours or until the beans are melt-in-your-mouth tender.* Adjust the seasonings.

5. Place a serving of rice on individual plates and top with a ladle of the piping hot beans. Serve as is or with a dash of hot sauce.

* If more water is needed during cooking, add it in small amounts only, as this dish is traditionally quite thick, not soupy.

FOR A CHANGE . . .

- Substitute a pinch or two of red pepper flakes for the cayenne pepper.
- Instead of dried thyme, add a spring of fresh. Remove the sprig before serving.
- For a quicker version, use 3 cans (15 ounces each) kidney beans instead of dried. Reduce the cooking time by 1 hour.

Asparagus-Chickpea-Brown Rice Stir-Fry

Looking for a quick and savory meal? Try this stir-fry made with leftover rice, fresh asparagus, and chickpeas . . . hearty and delicious!

1. Heat the oil in a large skillet over medium heat. Add the onion and garlic, and sauté for 2 to 3 minutes or until beginning to soften. Add the rice, chickpeas, and asparagus, and increase the heat to high. Stir-fry for 5 to7 minutes or until the ingredients are hot.

2. Transfer the rice mixture to a serving bowl and garnish with chopped nuts. Enjoy as is or topped with sauce.

FOR A CHANGE . . .

- Substitute fresh green beans or peas for the asparagus.
- Try lentils or black-eyed peas instead of chickpeas.

Yield: 4 to 6 servings

2 tablespoons extra virgin olive oil

1 cup chopped red onion

1 clove garlic, minced

4 cups cooked short-, medium-, or long-grain brown rice (page 19)

1 cup cooked chickpeas (rinse if canned)

2 cups cut asparagus (2-inch pieces), blanched

Chopped roasted hazelnuts, pecans, or slivered almonds for garnish

Tahini-Lemon Sauce (page 68)

Rice 'n Bean Enchiladas

Enchiladas are tortillas wrapped around a filling and baked in a spicy tomato or cream-style sauce. This vegan version is made with beans instead of the usual poultry or meat, and tofu sour cream instead of cheese. Because flour tortillas tend to get soggy, I prefer using corn tortillas. Be sure to lightly pan-fry the tortillas before filling to help prevent them from breaking.

Yield: 10 to 12 enchiladas

10 to 12 corn tortillas

2 tablespoons safflower oil

2 cups Tofu Sour Cream (page 74) or commercial variety

FILLING

2 cans (15 ounces each) vegetarian refried beans

2 cups cooked long-grain brown rice (page 19)

SAUCE

2 tablespoons safflower or extra virgin olive oil

1 medium onion, chopped

28-ounce can crushed tomatoes

1 cup Spicy Salsa (page 63) or commercial variety

1 small jalapeño pepper, seeded and minced

3 cloves garlic, minced

$1/2$ teaspoon ground cumin

$1/2$ teaspoon sea salt

$1/4$ teaspoon chili powder or taco seasoning

1 pinch red pepper flakes

1. To prepare the sauce, heat the oil in a medium skillet over medium-low heat. Add the onion, and sauté for 2 to 3 minutes or until beginning to soften. Add all of the remaining sauce ingredients, increase the heat, and bring almost to a boil. Reduce the heat to medium-low and cover. Simmer for 10 to 15 minutes. Remove from the heat and set aside.

2. While the sauce is simmering, heat half the safflower oil in a large skillet over medium-high heat. Add a tortilla, lightly fry for 1 minute, then turn over and lightly fry the other side. Fry another 4 or 5 tortillas. Heat the rest of the oil in the skillet, and fry the remaining tortillas.

3. Preheat the oven to 350°F. Spread about 1 cup of sauce on the bottom of a 13-x-9-inch baking dish and set aside.

4. Spread equal amounts of refried beans evenly on each tortilla, then top with equal amounts of rice. Roll up the tortillas and place them seam side down in the prepared baking dish. Spoon the remaining sauce on top. Pour the tofu cream across the middle of the enchiladas.

5. Bake for 30 to 35 minutes, or until the sauce is bubbling and the enchiladas are hot. Serve immediately.

FOR A CHANGE . . .

- Instead of filling the tortillas, layer the ingredients in an 8-inch square casserole dish. Spoon a layer of sauce on the bottom of the dish, then add a layer of tortillas, followed by layers of refried beans, rice, and tofu sour cream. Repeat the layers and bake as directed.

- Add 1 cup spaghetti sauce to the sauce ingredients for richer, thicker results.

Brown Rice and Bean Burritos

Burritos are often my go-to dinner when I have leftover rice and beans on hand. They're quick and easy to make, and always welcomed by my family.

1. Combine the rice and beans in a mixing bowl. Set aside.

2. Peel, pit, and slice the avocado. Set aside.

3. Place the burrito wrappers on a flat surface. Spread an equal amount of rice-and-bean mixture on each. Top with a lettuce leaf. On each leaf, place an equal amount of bell pepper slices, avocado slices, olives, and salsa.

4. Roll up the wrappers to enclose the filling. Serve as is or with extra salsa on the side.

FOR A CHANGE . . .

- Cut the burritos in half or quarters and serve as appetizers.

- Mix heated refried beans with any cooked rice or grain as a filling.

Yield: 6 burritos

$2^1/_2$ cups cooked short-, medium-, or long-grain brown rice (page 19)

$2^1/_2$ cups cooked pinto, black, or kidney beans (rinse if canned)

1 avocado

6 whole wheat burrito wrappers

6 large lettuce leaves (romaine, bib, Boston, and red leaf are recommended)

1 small bell pepper (any color), seeded and thinly sliced

$^1/_4$ cup pitted and sliced Kalamata or black olives

$^1/_2$ cup Spicy Salsa (page 63) or commercial variety

Brown Rice with Black-Eyed Peas & Seitan

Black-eyed peas served over rice is a Southern favorite.
This dish is often prepared with some type of meat.
This healthier version uses seitan instead.

Yield: 4 to 6 servings

2 cups long-grain brown rice, rinsed and drained

4 cups cold water

1 pinch sea salt

1 tablespoon extra virgin olive oil

1 cup diced red onion or shallots

1 clove garlic, minced

2 cans (15 ounces each) black-eyed peas, not drained

1 1/2 cups water

1 cup cubed seitan

1/4 cup diced celery

1/4 cup diced carrot

1/4 teaspoon black pepper

1/2 teaspoon sea salt

1 pinch red pepper flakes

Minced fresh parsley for garnish

1. Place the rice, water, and salt in a heavy medium-size pot. Cover and bring to a boil over high heat. Reduce the heat to medium-low, stir once, and cover. Simmer for 45 to 50 minutes or until the liquid is absorbed and the rice is tender.

2. While the rice is cooking, prepare the black-eyed peas. Heat the oil in a medium pot over medium-low heat. Add the onion, and sauté for 3 to 4 minutes or until beginning to soften. Add all of the remaining ingredients except the parsley, and bring to a boil over high heat.

3. Reduce the heat to medium-low, cover, and simmer for 20 to 25 minutes or until the vegetables are tender.

4. Transfer half the bean mixture to a blender and purée until smooth and creamy. Return to the pot, stir, and continue to simmer another 10 minutes.

5. Place a serving of rice on individual plates, and top with a ladle of black-eyed peas. Sprinkle with parsley and serve.

FOR A CHANGE . . .

● For a spark of heat, add 1/4 teaspoon hot pepper sesame oil to the black-eyed peas as they simmer. Or serve with your favorite hot sauce.

Spaghetti with Mushroom Marinara

Fresh pasta topped with succulent mushrooms in a rich tomato sauce is an Italian favorite. This basic recipe only gets better when you add your own favorite herbs and spices.

1. Heat the oil in a medium pot over medium heat. Add the onion and garlic, and sauté for 2 to 3 minutes or until beginning to soften. Add the mushrooms, and sauté for 2 to 3 minutes or until they release their juice.

2. Add the sauce and basil to the pot, cover, and bring to a boil over high heat. Reduce the heat to medium-low, cover, and simmer for 15 to 20 minutes while stirring occasionally.

3. While the sauce is simmering, cook the pasta according to package directions. Drain and transfer to a serving platter. Top with the hot sauce and serve.

FOR A CHANGE . . .

- For a spicier flavor, add a pinch of red pepper flakes to the sauce as it simmers.
- For added flavor, color, and texture, add chopped zucchini and/or yellow summer squash to the sauce.

Yield: 4 to 6 servings

3 tablespoons extra virgin olive oil

1 cup chopped onion

2 cloves garlic, minced

1 cup chopped button mushrooms

1 cup chopped crimini mushrooms

25-ounce jar spaghetti sauce, or 3 cups homemade

1 tablespoon chopped fresh basil

16 ounces brown rice spaghetti or udon noodles

A Little Rice Trivia . . .

After corn, rice is the grain with the highest worldwide production—over 400 million tons.

Rice & Bean Burgers

*I can always count on these burgers doing a quick
disappearing act at the dinner table. With my family,
there are never any leftovers.*

Yield: 4 to 6 servings

1 cup cubed buttercup squash or
Hokkaido pumpkin

3 to 4 cups any cooked
brown rice-and-bean combination

$1/2$ cup finely diced red onion

$1/2$ cup finely diced bell pepper
(any color)

$1/3$ cup fresh or frozen sweet corn

$1/4$ cup whole wheat bread crumbs
or whole wheat flour

2 tablespoons minced fresh parsley

1 clove garlic, minced

Safflower oil for frying burgers

1. Place the squash in a small pot with about an inch of water. Bring to a boil, cover the pot, and reduce the heat to low. Steam the squash for 4 to 5 minutes or until tender. Drain and place in a large mixing bowl.

2. Add all of the remaining ingredients except the safflower oil to the bowl. Mix the ingredients together with your hands, making sure to mash the squash well. Form the mixture into 8 to 12 burgers about 3 inches wide and $1/2$ inch thick.

3. Heat 3 to 4 tablespoons of oil in a large skillet over medium-high heat. Cook the burgers for 3 to 5 minutes on each side or until golden brown and crisp. Add more oil to the skillet as needed.

4. Serve the burgers as they are or on whole wheat buns. Top with your favorite condiments and garnishes. I usually serve them with Tahini-Lemon Sauce (page 68).

Rice is nice . . .
to help cool you down.

Fill a tube sock with raw rice, seal it with a rubber band, and toss it in the freezer. Place this "r-ice" pack against sprains or bruises to help reduce swelling, or lay it across your forehead to help ease a headache. When this cold pack becomes warm, pop it back in the freezer to use time and time again.

Vegetable Chow Mein

*My version of this popular Chinese dish contains
a nice variety of vegetables and is served
over crisp brown rice noodles.*

1. Bring the water to boil in a medium pot over high heat. Add the onion, cauliflower, broccoli, carrots, bean sprouts, bell pepper, celery, and water chestnuts. Cook 2 to 3 minutes or until the vegetables are partially cooked.

2. Dissolve the kuzu in the cold water.

3. Reduce the heat under the pot to low, add the dissolved kuzu, and stir constantly for 2 to 3 minutes or until the sauce thickens. Add the shoyu and ginger, and continue to cook another 1 to 2 minutes.

4. Ladle the piping hot chow mein over individual servings of crispy noodles.

FOR A CHANGE . . .

- Serve the chow mein over cooked brown or white rice instead of noodles.
- Use other quick-cooking vegetables, such as yellow summer squash, bok choy, snow peas, and snap peas.
- For a spicier flavor, add a sprinkle of cayenne pepper or a splash of hot sauce to the vegetables as they cook.

Yield: 4 to 6 servings

4 cups water

1 1/2 cups onion wedges
(1/2-inch thick)

1 cup small cauliflower florets

1 cup small broccoli florets

1/2 cup julienned carrots

1/2 cup fresh bean sprouts

1/3 cup chopped red bell pepper

1/4 cup sliced celery

1/4 cup sliced water chestnuts

5 tablespoons kuzu root starch

6 tablespoons cold water

1 1/2 tablespoons shoyu soy sauce,
or 1 teaspoon sea salt

1 tablespoon finely grated
fresh ginger

Crispy Rice Noodles (page 85)

Brown Rice & Quinoa Stuffed Peppers

*Stuffed peppers are filling, delicious, and easy to make.
They're also great for using up leftover brown rice.
The combination of grains and beans is especially nice.
Whether slow-simmered or baked, stuffed peppers
are always tender and flavorful.*

**Yield: 4 to 6
stuffed peppers**

4 to 6 medium green, red, yellow,
or orange bell peppers

1 $1/4$ cups spaghetti sauce

1 cup water

FILLING

1 cup cooked long-grain brown rice
or basmati (page 19)

1 cup cooked red quinoa

2 cups cooked pinto beans
(rinse if canned)

2 tablespoons safflower or
extra virgin olive oil

$1/2$ cup diced onion

2 cloves garlic, minced

$1/3$ cup fresh or frozen sweet corn

$1/2$ teaspoon ground cumin

$1/2$ teaspoon dried basil

$1/4$ teaspoon dried oregano

$1/4$ teaspoon sea salt

$1/8$ teaspoon black pepper

1. Slice the tops off the peppers and remove the seeds.

2. To prepare the filling, combine the rice, quinoa, and beans in a medium mixing bowl. Set aside.

3. Heat the oil in a medium skillet over medium heat. Add the onion and garlic, sauté for 2 to 3 minutes, then add to the rice mixture along with the remaining filling ingredients. Mix well.

4. Stuff each pepper with filling, then place in a heavy medium-size pot.

5. Mix the spaghetti sauce with the water. Pour half in the bottom of the pot, and the other half over the peppers. Cover and cook over low heat for $3\frac{1}{2}$ to 4 hours or until the peppers are tender. Check the cooking liquid periodically. If it evaporates, add more water and/or sauce to prevent burning.

6. Cool the stuffed peppers slightly before serving. Enjoy them plain or with a drizzle of cooking sauce.

FOR A CHANGE . . .

● Substitute other beans for the pinto. Black, kidney, and small red beans are good choices.

● Use wild rice instead of quinoa.

- Add $^1/_4$ cup finely chopped Kalamata olives to the filling.
- Instead of simmering the peppers in a pot on the stove, place them in a baking dish, cover, and bake in a 350°F oven for 1 to $1^1/_2$ hours.
- To reduce cooking time by almost half, blanch the peppers before stuffing.

Indonesian Peanut Pasta

This Southeast Asian staple is quick and easy to make, and offers a variety of delightful flavors and textures.

1. Cook the pasta according to package directions. Drain and set aside.

2. Heat the oil in a wok or large skillet over medium-high heat. Add the onion, and stir-fry for 3 to 4 minutes or until beginning to brown. Add the carrots and garlic, and stir-fry another minute.

3. Mix together the ginger, pepper flakes, and shoyu. Add to the wok along with the scallions, bean sprouts, snow peas, and pasta. Quickly stir-fry for 3 to 4 minutes or until the pasta is hot and the vegetables are bright and crisp.

4. Transfer to a serving bowl, sprinkle with peanuts, and enjoy.

Yield: 3 to 4 servings

12 ounces brown rice vermicelli or udon noodles

2 tablespoons peanut or extra virgin olive oil

2 cups coarsely chopped onion

$^1/_2$ cup julienned carrots

3 cloves garlic, minced

2 teaspoons finely grated fresh ginger

1 pinch red pepper flakes, or 2 dashes hot pepper sauce

$1^1/_2$ tablespoons shoyu soy sauce

3 scallions, cut into 2-inch lengths

1 cup fresh bean sprouts

1 cup snow peas, stems removed

Chopped unsalted roasted peanuts for garnish

Pad Thai

This spicy rice noodle dish is a Southeast Asian staple
that offers a variety of flavors and textures.

Yield: 3 to 4 servings

8 ounces brown rice udon noodles
or vermicelli

$^1/_4$ cup fresh lime juice

2 tablespoons maple syrup or honey

2 tablespoons shoyu soy sauce

$1^1/_2$ tablespoons water

2 teaspoons finely grated
fresh ginger

2 teaspoons extra virgin olive oil

$1^1/_2$ teaspoons hot pepper
sesame oil or chili oil

2 large garlic cloves, minced

1 cup julienned carrots

1 cup fresh bean sprouts

1 cup chopped Chinese cabbage

3 scallions, cut into 2-inch lengths

$^1/_2$ cup snow peas or snap peas,
stems removed

2 tablespoons finely chopped
fresh parsley

Chopped unsalted roasted peanuts
for garnish

1. Cook the noodles according to package directions. Rinse, drain, and set aside.

2. Combine the lime juice, maple syrup, shoyu, water, and ginger in a small bowl. Set aside.

3. Heat the oils in a wok or large skillet over medium heat. Add the garlic and sauté for 1 minute. Increase the heat to medium-high, add the carrots, and stir-fry 2 minutes. Add the bean sprouts and stir-fry another minute.

4. Add the lime juice mixture to the wok along with the cabbage, scallions, snow peas, and cooked noodles. Continue to cook 2 to 3 minutes or until the vegetables are tender yet crisp, and the noodles are hot.

5. Toss the parsley with the noodles and transfer to a serving bowl. Garnish with peanuts and serve.

FOR A CHANGE . . .

- Substitute small broccoli florets or bok choy for the Chinese cabbage.
- Add $^1/_2$ cup sliced fresh shiitake mushroom caps.
- For added crunch, add $^1/_4$ cup water chestnuts.

9

Desserts and Treats

When it comes to desserts and sweet treats, "healthy" isn't a word that usually comes to mind. Most products, especially commercial varieties, are highly processed, made with refined flour and hydrogenated oil, as well as chemical preservatives, flavorings, and other additives. Their sweetness comes from refined sugar, high fructose corn syrup, or artificial sweeteners.

The healthier alternatives in this chapter are made with whole grain brown rice and other natural ingredients. They are sweetened with products like pure maple syrup, honey, brown rice syrup, and fruit—both fresh and dried.

The Applesauce Brown Rice Muffins are moist and sweet, and the ones most requested by my family. The heavenly Banana-Nut Muffins, with their incomparable flavor and walnut-ty crunch, are also winners. If you're a fan of rice pudding, you'll enjoy the simple yet satisfying Brown Rice Pudding—it is rich and creamy with a hint of cinnamon. The maple-sweetened Quinoa Fruit Pudding is another exceptional choice. And be sure to try the Brown Rice Cake S'mores—a healthier version of the traditional campfire treat.

In Japan, sweet brown rice is used to make a number of the country's traditional sweet treats like ohagi. Ohagi are golf ball-sized rounds or nuggets of partially pounded sweet rice that are covered in a coating of ground nuts or seeds. Recipes for Walnut Ohagi and Chestnut Ohagi are included in this chapter, as well as other dishes made with sweet brown rice.

All of the treats in this chapter are healthful and easy to prepare. Best of all, they taste great and are guaranteed to satisfy even your strongest dessert cravings.

Applesauce
Brown Rice Muffins

Moist and sweet, these muffins are a real family favorite.
The combination of unbleached white and whole wheat
pastry flour adds to their lightness.

Yield: 12 muffins

I cup unbleached white flour

I cup whole wheat pastry flour

I cup cooked short-, medium-,
or long-grain brown or white rice
(page 19)

I tablespoon baking powder

I teaspoon baking soda

I teaspoon cinnamon

$^1/_4$ teaspoon sea salt

$^3/_4$ cup plain unsweetened soymilk

2 teaspoons apple cider vinegar

I tablespoon safflower oil

I cup applesauce

$^1/_3$ cup maple syrup

I teaspoon vanilla

1. Preheat the oven to 375° F. Lightly oil a standard 12-cup muffin tin and set aside.

2. Combine the white flour, pastry flour, rice, baking powder, baking soda, cinnamon, and salt in a medium mixing bowl. Set aside.

3. Place the soymilk, vinegar, and oil in a small bowl and stir well. Let sit for 5 minutes or until curds form. Add the applesauce, maple syrup, and vanilla, and stir well.

4. Add the soymilk-applesauce mixture to the flour mixture and stir until just blended. Do not overstir.

5. Spoon the batter into the prepared muffin tin, filling each cup about $^3/_4$ full.

6. Bake for 20 to 25 minutes, or until a toothpick inserted into the center of a muffin comes out clean.

7. Remove from the oven. Let the muffins cool at least 10 minutes before removing from the tin. Serve warm or at room temperature.

Banana-Nut Brown Rice Muffins

Mixing cooked brown rice into the batter results in a moist, nutritious muffin with added fiber.

1. Preheat the oven to 375° F. Lightly oil a standard 12-cup muffin tin and set aside.

2. Combine the flour, rice, baking powder, and salt in a medium mixing bowl. Set aside.

3. Place the soy buttermilk, water, syrup, and vanilla in a small bowl or measuring cup, and stir well.

4. Add the soymilk mixture to the flour mixture and stir until just blended. Fold the banana, walnuts, and raisins into the batter. Mix but do not overstir.

5. Spoon the batter into the prepared muffin tin, filling each cup about ³/₄ full.

6. Bake for 20 to 25 minutes, or until a toothpick inserted into the center of a muffin comes out clean.

7. Remove from the oven. Let the muffins cool at least 10 minutes before removing from the tin. Serve warm or at room temperature.

Yield: 12 muffins

2¹/₂ cups whole wheat pastry flour

I cup cooked short-, medium-, or long-grain brown rice (page 19)

I tablespoon baking powder

¹/₂ teaspoon sea salt

1¹/₄ cups Soy Buttermilk* (page 72)

³/₄ cup water

¹/₃ cup maple syrup

I teaspoon vanilla

2 cups ripe mashed banana

I cup chopped walnuts

¹/₂ cup raisins

* Instead of soy buttermilk, you can use 1 medium egg and 1¹/₄ cups plain soymilk.

A Little Rice Trivia . . .

The average American eats about 25 pounds of rice per year, while in Asia, the average is closer to 300 pounds.

Amazake Lemon Pudding

Creamy and sweet, this dessert is especially ideal
for those who are allergic to dairy products.

Yield: 3 to 4 servings

4 heaping teaspoons
kuzu root starch

5 teaspoons cold water

4 cups (1 quart) amazake

1 teaspoon lemon zest

Fresh raspberries or blueberries
for garnish

Chopped roasted walnuts, pecans,
or hazelnuts for garnish

1. Dissolve the kuzu in the cold water, then place in a medium pot along with the amazake. Bring to a boil over medium-high heat while stirring frequently. Reduce the heat to low, and simmer while continuing to stir for 1 to 2 minutes or until the mixture thickens.

2. Remove from the heat, add the lemon zest, and mix well. Spoon into individual bowls and serve at room temperature, or refrigerate and enjoy chilled. Garnish with berries and nuts before serving.

FOR A CHANGE . . .

- For added flavor, include 1 tablespoon instant grain coffee in Step 1.
- Garnish the pudding with a sprinkling of Granola (page 35).
- In addition to the lemon zest, add 1 tablespoon dark cocoa powder.
- For a spicy kick, add a dash of ground cinnamon, nutmeg, or ginger along with the lemon zest.

AMAZAKE

Amazake is a fermented non-alcoholic, gluten-free beverage made from sweet brown rice or short-grain brown rice. In addition to being enjoyed as a sweet drink, amazake is often used in puddings, custards, and other desserts. You can also pour it over hot or cold cereals as you would dairy milk, soymilk, or rice milk. It is somewhat thicker than other types of milk, but can be mixed with water, rice milk, or soymilk to the desired thickness and sweetness. Prepared amazake is sold in the dairy section of most natural foods stores.

Brown Rice Pudding

Quick and easy to make, this pudding is great for using up leftover rice—short-grain is best for the creamiest results.

Yield: 4 to 5 servings

2 cups cooked short-grain brown rice (page 19)

2 cups vanilla soymilk

$^1/_2$ cup raisins or dried cranberries

2 tablespoons maple syrup

1 teaspoon vanilla

$^1/_2$ teaspoon lemon zest

$^1/_4$ teaspoon ground cinnamon

1. Place the rice, soymilk, raisins, and maple syrup in a medium pot. Cover and bring to a boil over medium heat. Reduce the heat to medium-low, and simmer 15 to 20 minutes or until creamy.

2. Add all of the remaining ingredients, and continue to simmer another 5 minutes.

3. Serve at room temperature or enjoy chilled.

FOR A CHANGE . . .

- For richer flavor, add 2 tablespoons cashew or almond butter in Step 1.

Quinoa Fruit Pudding

This rich, satisfying dessert gets its smooth creaminess from rice and pleasant mild crunch from quinoa.

Yield: 4 to 5 servings

2 cups cooked short-grain brown rice (page 19)

1 cup cooked white quinoa

$2^1/_2$ cups vanilla soymilk

$^1/_2$ cup chopped apples

2 tablespoons maple syrup

1 teaspoon vanilla

1 teaspoon ground cinnamon

Fresh blueberries for garnish

Slivered almonds for garnish

1. Place the rice, quinoa, and soymilk in a medium pot. Cover and bring to a boil over medium heat. Reduce the heat to medium-low, and simmer for 10 to 15 minutes or until soft and creamy.

2. Add the apples, maple syrup, vanilla, and cinnamon. Cover and continue to simmer another 5 to 8 minutes or until the apples are soft.

3. Serve at room temperature or enjoy chilled. Garnish with blueberries and almonds before serving.

Sweet Rice Nuggets

Dried fruit offers added sweetness to these nuggets,
while nuts provide richness and crunch.

Yield: 16 to 20 nuggets

1 cup short-grain brown rice, rinsed and drained

1 cup sweet brown rice, rinsed and drained

4 cups cold water

1 pinch sea salt

1 cup raisins, currants, or dried blueberries

2 cups coarsely chopped roasted walnuts, pecans, hazelnuts, or almonds

1. Place both rice varieties, the water, and salt in a heavy medium-size pot. Cover and bring to a boil over high heat. Reduce the heat to medium-low, stir once, and cover. Simmer for 45 to 50 minutes or until the liquid is absorbed and the rice is tender.

2. Remove from the heat and let sit 10 minutes, then transfer to a medium mixing bowl. Fold the raisins into the rice and let cool.

3. Moisten your hands slightly with cold water, then form the rice mixture into golf ball-sized rounds.

4. Roll the balls in the chopped nuts to completely coat, arrange on a platter, and serve. Store leftovers in an airtight container in the refrigerator for one or two days.

FOR A CHANGE . . .

• Substitute coarsely ground roasted sesame, sunflower, or pumpkin seeds for the nuts.

• Dip the balls in maple syrup or hot rice syrup before rolling in nuts.

A Little Rice Trivia . . .

Two Japanese car brands—Toyota and Honda—are named after rice. *Toyota* translates to "Bountiful Rice Field," while *Honda* means "Main Rice Field."

OHAGI

Ohagi is the Japanese name for small nuggets of partially pounded sweet rice. They are typically coated with coarsely ground seasoned nuts or seeds, such as the Walnut Ohagi on page 169, or encased in a thick rich coating, like the Chestnut Ohagi on page 168.

Traditionally, the cooked rice is hand pounded with a wooden pestle, although pulsing it for several seconds in a food processor is a quick and easy option. Ohagi make great snacks and appetizers, and can serve as the main grain for brunch, lunch, or dinner. As an added bonus, they can be made ahead of time, stored in a covered container, and refrigerated for several days.

Sweet Brown Rice

Stickier than regular short-grain brown rice, sweet brown rice is higher in protein and B vitamins than most rice varieties. In Japan, it is traditionally used to make brown rice vinegar, sake (rice wine), amazake (a sweet non-alcoholic beverage), and mochi rice cakes. You can enjoy sweet brown rice in its simple cooked state (as in this recipe), combine it with other grains, or enjoy it in puddings and other and Asian-style treats.

Yield: 2½ to 3 cups

I cup sweet brown rice, rinsed and drained

2 cups water

I pinch sea salt

1. Place all of the ingredients in a heavy medium-size pot. Cover and bring to a boil over high heat. Reduce the heat to medium-low, stir once, and simmer for 45 to 50 minutes or until the liquid is absorbed and the rice is tender.

2. Remove from the heat and let sit for 10 minutes.

3. Best served warm. When cold, sweet brown rice is commonly used to make ohagi—a sweet Japanese treat (see above).

Chestnut Ohagi

Dried chestnuts are often ground into flour and used to make cookies, pie crusts, and other baked goods. They are also cooked whole and then tossed into salads or added to vegetable dishes. In this recipe, they are turned into a thick creamy paste that is used as a delicious covering for ohagi. Dried chestnuts are available in most natural foods stores and Asian and Italian specialty markets.

Yield: 35 to 40 ohagi

1 cup dried chestnuts, rinsed and drained

3 cups cold water

1 pinch sea salt

1 recipe Sweet Brown Rice (page 167)

1. Place the chestnuts and water in a small saucepan, cover, and let soak 6 to 8 hours or overnight.

2. Add the salt to the soaked chestnuts, cover, and bring to a boil over high heat. Reduce the heat to medium-low, cover, and simmer about $1^1/_2$ hours or until tender.

3. Reserving the cooking water, drain the chestnuts and place in a medium mixing bowl. Mash with a potato masher, adding a small amount of reserved cooking water, to form a thick paste-like mixture that can hold a shape. Set aside.

4. Place the rice in a food processor and pulse several times until the grains are half crushed and sticky. (If you do not have a food processor, you can omit this step.) Transfer to a bowl and set aside.

5. Moisten your hands slightly with cold water. Take about 1 tablespoon of the chestnut mixture and form it into a golf ball-sized round. Press a hole into the center of the ball with your finger. Add 1 or 2 teaspoons of sweet rice in the center, then pack up the ball again to close the hole.

6. Repeat until all ohagi are formed. Arrange on a platter and serve.

FOR A CHANGE . . .

- To save time, you can pressure-cook the soaked chestnuts, which will take about 45 minutes.

- Instead of mashing the cooked chestnuts by hand, you can use a stick blender or food processor.

Walnut Ohagi

Rich and nutty with a slight saltiness from shoyu,
this ohagi is my favorite.

1. Place the walnuts and soy sauce in a food processor and pulse several seconds until coarsely ground. *Do not over grind.* Transfer to a small bowl and set aside.

2. Place the cooked rice in the food processor and pulse several times until the grains are half crushed and sticky. (If you do not have a food processor, you can omit this step.)

3. Moisten your hands slightly with cold water, then form the rice mixture into golf ball-sized rounds.

4. Roll the balls in the ground nuts to completely coat, then flatten slightly between your palms into $1/2$-inch-thick circles. Arrange on a platter and serve.

> Yield: 35 to 40 ohagi
>
> I cup roasted walnuts
>
> I teaspoon shoyu soy sauce
>
> I recipe Sweet Brown Rice (page 167)

FOR A CHANGE . . .

- Instead of soy sauce, use $1/4$ teaspoon sea salt.

- Substitute roasted pecans, hazelnuts, cashews, or almonds for the walnuts.

- Coat the ohagi in roasted sesame, sunflower, or pumpkin seeds instead of nuts. Also, use only $1/2$ teaspoon soy sauce.

Sweet Rice and Chestnuts

In this recipe, sweet brown rice is cooked together with dried chestnuts. It's a delightful treat that is especially nice to serve on Thanksgiving and other end-of-the-year holidays.

Yield: 3 to 4 servings

¹/₂ cup dried chestnuts, rinsed and drained

2 cups cold water

I cup sweet brown rice, rinsed and drained

I pinch sea salt

1. Heat a medium skillet over medium-low heat. Add the chestnuts and dry-roast 5 to 7 minutes, stirring constantly, until they release a sweet aroma and begin to turn golden. Be careful not to burn.

2. Transfer the chestnuts to a heavy medium-size pot along with the water and rice. Cover and let soak for 1 to 2 hours.

3. Add the salt to the soaked rice and chestnuts, cover, and bring to a boil. Reduce the heat to medium-low, stir once, and cover. Simmer for 50 to 60 minutes, or until the liquid is absorbed and the rice and chestnuts are tender.

4. Remove from the heat and let sit 10 minutes. Transfer to a serving bowl and enjoy warm or at room temperature.

FOR A CHANGE . . .

● Instead of cooking this dish on the stovetop, you can use a pressure cooker. Reduce the water to 1¹/₂ cups and cook the soaked chestnuts and rice for 40 to 45 minutes.

Brown Rice Cake S'mores

No matter how old you are, s'mores will make you feel like a kid again. In this recipe, brown rice cakes replace the traditional graham crackers, while nut butter adds a new flavor to this time-honored campfire treat.

1. Preheat the oven to 300°F.

2. Add the rice syrup to the peanut butter and stir until the mixture is well blended. Spread a thick layer on top of 3 rice cakes.

3. Sprinkle chocolate chips and marshmallows on top of the peanut butter. Cover with the remaining rice cakes.

4. Arrange the rice cakes on a baking sheet, and bake 5 to 7 minutes or until the chocolate melts. Be careful not to burn. Serve warm.

FOR A CHANGE . . .

- Use slices of banana instead of or in addition to the mini marshmallows.

Yield: 3 s'mores

6 brown rice cakes

$1/2$ cup peanut, cashew, or almond butter

1 tablespoon brown rice syrup

$1/2$ cup semi-sweet chocolate chips

$1/3$ cup mini marshmallows*

* I recommend vegan marshmallows as an alternative to sugary sweet ones.

Rice is nice . . . to help bake pies.

When prebaking a pie crust, place a sheet of baking parchment or foil over the unbaked crust, then top with a few handfuls of raw rice to weigh it down. This weight will prevent the crust from bubbling up and blistering as it bakes.

Deep-Fried Mochi Puffs

These mochi puffs are delicious just as they are, although you can drizzle them with your favorite sweet or savory sauce. I even enjoy them as croutons for soup.

Yield: About 15 puffs

5 to 6 ounces fresh brown rice mochi, cut into 1-inch squares

Safflower oil for deep-frying

1. Heat 2 to 3 inches of oil in a deep fryer or a heavy medium-size pot. Add 3 or 4 squares of mochi, and deep-fry for 3 to 5 minutes or until puffed up and golden. Remove and place on paper towels to absorb any oil. Repeat with the remaining mochi.

2. Serve the puffs immediately, as mochi tends to become hard shortly after it is cooked.

ABOUT MOCHI

A Japanese staple sold almost exclusively in natural foods stores and Asian markets, mochi is made from cooked sweet rice that has been pounded and formed into dense cakes. Brown rice mochi is available fresh or vacuum packaged in dried dense slabs. White rice mochi is usually sold fresh.

Mochi can be pan-fried with or without oil, deep-fried, baked, or steamed. When cooked, this mildly sweet cake puffs up, becoming crisp on the outside and soft and sticky on the inside. It is also fairly versatile. Commonly enjoyed as a sweet confection either plain or drizzled with syrup, mochi also makes a great savory snack when topped with a sprinkle of soy sauce or served with a spicy dip. It can be cooked in a waffle iron and enjoyed for breakfast (see Mochi Waffles on page 36), or grated and served as a garnish over hot soup (see French Onion Soup on page 54).

These are just a few of the many ways in which you can incorporate this delicious food into your diet. Let the experimenting begin!

Sweet 'n Nutty Mochi Squares

Rich and chewy, this popular Japanese treat is really easy to make. It's always welcomed in my home.

1. Cut the mochi into 6 pieces (2-inch squares). Set aside.

2. Heat a heavy medium-size skillet over medium-high heat. Add the mochi, cover, and reduce the heat to low. Cook 3 to 5 minutes or until slightly browned on the bottom. Flip the pieces over, cover, and cook another 5 minutes or until the mochi puffs up and is slightly browned. Be careful not to burn.

3. While the mochi is cooking, heat the syrup in a small saucepan and keep hot.

4. Dip each piece of cooked mochi in the hot syrup, then roll in the chopped nuts to completely coat. Serve immediately, as mochi tends to become hard shortly after it is cooked.

FOR A CHANGE . . .

- Use fresh mochi (about 5 to 6 ounces) instead of dried.

- Instead of nuts, roll the mochi in toasted whole or ground sesame seeds or Gomashio (page 67).

- For a more savory version, eliminate the syrup and nuts, and wrap the cooked mochi in pieces of toasted nori. Dip in shoyu soy sauce before eating.

- Oven bake the mochi at 350°F for 7 to 10 minutes or until puffed up and lightly browned.

Yield: 6 squares

10.5-ounce package dried brown rice mochi

1/4 cup brown rice syrup, maple syrup, or honey

1/3 cup finely chopped roasted walnuts, pecans, hazelnuts, or almonds

Metric Conversion Tables

COMMON LIQUID CONVERSIONS

Measurement	=	Milliliters
1/4 teaspoon	=	1.25 milliliters
1/2 teaspoon	=	2.50 milliliters
3/4 teaspoon	=	3.75 milliliters
1 teaspoon	=	5.00 milliliters
1 1/4 teaspoons	=	6.25 milliliters
1 1/2 teaspoons	=	7.50 milliliters
1 3/4 teaspoons	=	8.75 milliliters
2 teaspoons	=	10.0 milliliters
1 tablespoon	=	15.0 milliliters
2 tablespoons	=	30.0 milliliters

Measurement	=	Liters
1/4 cup	=	0.06 liters
1/2 cup	=	0.12 liters
3/4 cup	=	0.18 liters
1 cup	=	0.24 liters
1 1/4 cups	=	0.30 liters
1 1/2 cups	=	0.36 liters
2 cups	=	0.48 liters
2 1/2 cups	=	0.60 liters
3 cups	=	0.72 liters
3 1/2 cups	=	0.84 liters
4 cups	=	0.96 liters
4 1/2 cups	=	1.08 liters
5 cups	=	1.20 liters
5 1/2 cups	=	1.32 liters

CONVERTING FAHRENHEIT TO CELSIUS

Fahrenheit	=	Celsius
200–205	=	95
220–225	=	105
245–250	=	120
275	=	135
300–305	=	150
325–330	=	165
345–350	=	175
370–375	=	190
400–405	=	205
425–430	=	220
445–450	=	230
470–475	=	245
500	=	260

CONVERSION FORMULAS

LIQUID		
When You Know	Multiply By	To Determine
teaspoons	5.0	milliliters
tablespoons	15.0	milliliters
fluid ounces	30.0	milliliters
cups	0.24	liters
pints	0.47	liters
quarts	0.95	liters

WEIGHT		
When You Know	Multiply By	To Determine
ounces	28.0	grams
pounds	0.45	kilograms

Resources

To prepare the delicious dishes in this book, the use of high-quality ingredients—preferably organic and GMO-free—is recommended. Most of the products called for are readily available at natural foods stores and major supermarkets. If, however, you are unable to find a particular item, you can order it from one of the following well-established, reliable companies.

Bob's Red Mill
13521 SE Pheasant Court
Milwaukie, OR 97222
(503) 654-3215
(800) 349-2173
www.bobsredmill.com

Extensive line of stone-ground organic whole grains, whole grain products, nuts, and seeds.

Braga Organic Farms
10668 Road 26 1/2
Madera, CA 93637
(855) 661-2101
www.buyorganicnuts.com

Organic nuts—almonds, cashews, pistachios, and walnuts; nut butters; trail mix; and dried fruit.

Bionaturae
5 Tyler Drive
PO Box 98
North Franklin, CT 06254
(860) 642-6996
www.bionaturae.com

Tuscan-produced organic whole wheat pasta (including gluten-free varieties), olive oil, balsamic vinegar, and tomato products.

Coombs Family Farms
PO Box 117
Brattleboro, VT 05302
(888) 266-6271
www.coombsfamilyfarms.com

Organic pure maple syrup and other maple products.

Earthy Delights
1161 East Clark Road, Suite 260
DeWitt, MI 48820
(800) 367-4709
www.earthy.com

*Fresh wild mushrooms and other seasonal
wild harvested products.*

Eden Foods
701 Tecumseh Road
Clinton, MI 49236
(888) 424-3336
www.edenfoods.com

*Over 350 high-quality organic products, including a
full line of organic soymilks, whole grains and grain
flakes, dried and prepared beans, pastas, freshly
ground flours, nuts, seeds, dried fruit, oils, and
seasonings. Full line of macrobiotic products—sea
vegetables, miso, noodles, kuzu, mirin, dried shiitake
and maitake mushrooms, condiments, shoyu and
tamari soy sauce, and umeboshi products.*

Essential Living Foods
3550 Hayden Avenue
Culver City, CA 90232
(310) 319-1555
www.essentiallivingfoods.com

*Organic raw foods and "superfoods," including
chocolate, dried fruits, nuts and nut butters, seeds,
sweeteners, and herbs.*

Ferris Organic Farm
3565 Onondaga Road
Eaton Rapids, MI 48827
(800) 628-8736
www.ferrisorganicfarm.com

*Organic grains, beans, nuts, seeds, rice, and
freshly milled flours and meals.*

Frontier Natural Products Co-op
PO Box 299
3021 78th Street
Norway, IA 52318
(800) 669-3275
www.frontiercoop.com

*Natural and organic herbs and spices, seasoning
blends, and more.*

Gold Mine Natural Food Company
7805 Arjons Drive
San Diego, CA 92126
(800) 475-FOOD (3663)
www.goldminenaturalfoods.com

*Full line of organic and macrobiotic products—
whole grains and whole grain products, beans, oils,
sea vegetables, miso, dried fruits, noodles, nuts,
kuzu, mirin, dried shiitake and wild mushrooms,
sweeteners, and umeboshi products.*

Gourmet House Rice
c/o Riviana Consumer Relations
PO Box 90340
Allentown, PA 18109-0340
(800) 226-9522
www.gourmethouserice.com

*Organic brown and white rice, gourmet blends
including jasmine, Arborio, basmati, wild rice,
and wild rice blends.*

Great Eastern Sun
92 McIntosh Road
Asheville, NC 28806
(800) 334-5809
www.great-eastern-sun.com

*Traditional, organic, and macrobiotic foods,
including soba and udon noodles, wasabi and
other condiments, miso, and sea vegetables.*

Indian Harvest
PO Box 428
1012 Paul Bunyan Drive SE
Bemidji, MN 56619
(800) 346-7032
www.indianharvest.com

An extensive line of specialty rice, including Arborio, carnaroli, brown basmati, white basmati, Chinese bamboo rice, Chinese black rice, red rice, purple Thai, and red jasmine. Also wild rice, whole grains, multi-grain blends, and heirloom beans and lentils.

The Kushi Store
PO Box 500
308 Leland Road
Becket, MA 01223
(413) 623-6679
(800) 645-8744
www.kushistore.com

Organic whole grains, beans, nuts, seeds, dried mushrooms, sea vegetables, and macrobiotic staples.

Living Tree Community Foods
PO Box 10082
Berkeley, CA 94709
(510) 526-7106
(800) 260-5534
www.livingtreecommunity.com

Organic oils, nut and nut butters, sea vegetables, sweeteners, and more.

Lotus Foods
c/o WorldPantry.com, Inc.
1192 Illinois Street
San Francisco, CA 94107
(866) 972-6879
www.lotusfoods.com

Organic rice varieties, including brown basmati, Bhutanese red, and Chinese "forbidden" black.

Lundberg Family Farms
PO Box 369
5311 Midway
Richvale, CA 95974
(530) 538-3500
www.lundberg.com

Extensive line of organic/eco-farmed whole grain rice and rice blends, as well as rice products.

Mahatma
c/o Riviana Consumer Relations
PO Box 90340
Allentown, PA 18109
(800) 226-9522
www.mahatmarice.com

Whole grain and specialty rice varieties.

Maine Coast Sea Vegetables
3 George's Pond Road
Franklin, ME 04634
(207) 565-2907
www.seaveg.com

High-quality sea vegetables from the North Atlantic.

Mendocino Sea Vegetable Company
PO Box 455
Philo, CA 95466
(707) 895-2996
www.seaweed.net

High-quality sea vegetables from the Pacific.

MycoLogical Natural Products
PO Box 24940
Eugene, OR 97402
(888) 465-3247
www.mycological.com

Line of organic fresh and dried mushrooms, and dried chile peppers.

Natural Import Company
9 Reed Street, Suite A
Biltmore Village, NC 28803
(800) 324-1878
www.naturalimport.com

Traditionally made Japanese foods, including miso, mochi, kuzu, amazake, seitan, and dried tofu.

Nuts.com
125 Moen Street
Cranford, NJ 07016
(800) 558-6887
www.nuts.com

Organic grains, flours, nuts, seeds, and snacks.

OliveNation
50 Terminal Street
Building 2, 7th Floor
Charlestown, MA 02129
(781) 989-2033
www.olivenation.com

Imported specialty and gourmet rice varieties including Arborio, carnaroli, Chinese black, Himalayan red, sushi rice, basmati, jasmine, and more. Also, a full line of dried mushrooms, beans, grains, and seeds.

Purcell Mountain Farm
393 Firehouse Road
Moyie Springs, ID 83845
(208) 267-0627
www.purcellmountainfarms.com

Organic brown rice (including specialty varieties), grains and grain products, and beans/legumes.

Rice Select
13100 Space Center Boulevard
Houston, TX 77059
(800) 993-RICE (7423)
www.riceselect.com

Organic Texmati rice varieties, whole grain Texmati blends, Arborio rice, and whole wheat couscous.

Sun Organic Farm
411 South Las Posas Road
San Marcos, CA 92078
(760) 510-8077
(888) 269-9888
www.sunorganicfarm.com

A complete line of certified organic rice, brown rice pastas, flours, whole grains, beans, seeds, nuts, dried fruits, sweeteners, and more.

South River Miso
888 Shelburne Falls Road
Conway, MA 01341
(413) 369-4057
www.southrivermiso.com

Hand-crafted, wood-fired, certified organic miso, made according to a centuries-old time-honored Japanese farmhouse tradition.

Tinkyáda
c/o Food Directions, Inc.
120 Melford Drive, Unit 8
Scarborough, Ontario
M1B 2X5 Canada
(416) 609-0016
(888) 323-2388
www.ricepasta.com
www.tinkyada.com

Organic brown rice pasta varieties—spaghetti, elbows, penne, spirals, and lasagna.

Village Harvest
c/o Otis McAllister, Inc.
160 Pine Street, Suite 350
San Francisco, CA 94111
(415) 421-6010
www.villageharvestrice.com

Imported line of natural and organic brown rice and white rice varieties, including basmati, jasmine, Arborio, and sushi rice. Also offer frozen precooked whole grains and grain blends.

Index

SQUAREONE'S NATURAL FOODS COOKBOOKS

$17.95 US • 320 pages
7.5 x 9-inch quality paperback
ISBN 978-0-7570-0251-9

$16.95 US • 240 pages
7.5 x 9-inch quality paperback
ISBN 978-0-7570-0091-1

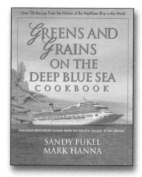

$16.95 US • 160 pages
7.5 x 9-inch quality paperback
ISBN 978-0-7570-0287-8

$15.95 US • 144 pages
7.5 x 9-inch quality paperback
ISBN 978-0-7570-0346-2

$18.95 US • 240 pages
8 x 10-inch quality paperback
ISBN 978-1-890612-45-0

$18.95 US • 240 pages
7.5 x 9-inch quality paperback
ISBN 978-0-7570-0385-1

$16.95 US • 248 pages
7.5 x 9-inch quality paperback
ISBN 978-0-7570-0273-1

$14.95 US • 288 pages
6 x 9-inch quality paperback
ISBN 978-0-7570-0266-3

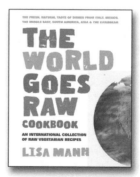

$16.95 US • 176 pages
7.5 x 9-inch quality paperback
ISBN 978-0-7570-0320-2

**For more information about our books,
visit our website at www.squareonepublishers.com**